**Stuff**

Birth to 8

Selecting Play N̶ ̶ ̶ ̶ ̶ ̶ ̶ ̶ ̶ ̶nent

**Martha B. Bronson**

National Association for the Education of Young Children, Washington, D.C.

*Illustrations:* Lura Schwarz Smith

**National Association for the Education
  of Young Children**
**1509 16th Street, N.W.**
**Washington, DC 20036-1426**
**202-232-8777 or 1-800-424-2460**

The National Association for the Education of Young Children (NAEYC) attempts through its publications program to provide a forum for discussion of major issues and ideas in our field. We hope to provoke thought and promote professional growth. The views expressed or implied are not necessarily those of the Association. NAEYC wishes to thank the author, who donated much time and effort to develop this book as a contribution to our profession.

Library of Congress Catalog Card Number: 95-072388
ISBN Catalog Number: 0-935989-72-2
NAEYC #312

*Editor:* Carol Copple; *Book design/production:* Jack Zibulsky, Danielle Hudson, Penny Atkins; *Copyediting:* Betty Nylund Barr; *Editorial assistance:* Anika Trahan, Jill Kaufman

**Printed in the United States of America.**

# Contents

# About the Author

**Martha Berger Bronson,** Ed.D., is an assistant professor of developmental and educational psychology and early childhood education at the Boston College School of Education. She co-authored, with Barbara Dillon Goodson of Abt Associates, the U.S. Consumer Product Safety Commission's *Guidelines for Relating Children's Ages to Toy Characteristics* and two booklets for consumers on selecting toys for children from birth through age 12. Martha has been a teacher of children ages 3 through 5 and the director of a school for this age group. Her research has also taken her into hundreds of early childhood classrooms. She has been very involved in developing appropriate ways to assess social and mastery skills in young children, and her observational measures have been used in national studies. She has a complementary interest in how play materials support social and mastery development.

# Acknowledgments

I would like to acknowledge first the contribution of Barbara Goodson of Abt Associates. Our work together, which produced the *Guidelines for Relating Children's Ages to Toy Characteristics* for the Consumer Product Safety Commission, laid the groundwork for this book. In addition, I want to express my gratitude to Carol Copple for her thoughtful comments and wise, helpful guidance at every stage of the book's development. I would also like to thank Betty Nylund Barr for her careful copyediting and skillful management of a multitude of tiny details. Finally, I want to thank my husband for his unfailing support, and to thank my children, grandchildren, and the thousands of children I have observed in their classrooms for the inspiration of their play.

# Introduction

Many animals play, but primates play more, and humans play the most (Eibl-Eibesfeldt 1970; Bruner 1976). The amount and complexity of play increases as creatures become progressively more dependent on learning rather than on instinctual programming for survival. The human species needs the most learning and continues to play throughout the lifespan. We not only play spontaneously, we seem to have a need to play (Smith 1984; Ellis 1988).

The child's play interests reveal many of the interests of humankind (Piaget 1963; Vygotsky 1976). We are curious about the social and physical world and reach out to explore it. We manipulate and experiment to see what will happen and how things and people function. We try to master and control processes and produce desired effects by our own efforts. We also imitate what we perceive, and we play with these images in spontaneous variations on the captured themes.

We play in a wide variety of situations and using a broad range of our physical and mental capacities. We play alone or with others, with objects and with ideas. Beyond simple use of our motor abilities, we create detailed and complex elaborations and refinements, such as dance and sport. We play with each of our senses separately and together, inventing new ways to see, hear, smell, taste, and touch the world.

Human play is characteristically imaginative and symbolic (Piaget 1962; Werner & Kaplan 1963). We play with the connections and associations in our minds, creating patterns that both mimic and create reality, from fantasy and art to philosophy and science. We play with social roles and rules, fashioning conventions and styles of interaction that generate and change cultural patterns. We play with our appearance with paint and dress, constructing fanciful, fantastic, or fearful images. We even play with our own identities, trying out roles and fabricating personas, in endless invention.

Children's desire and need to play has been recognized throughout history (Borstelmann 1983), but it is not only children who explore and experiment, imagine and play with symbols, and enjoy manipulating the social and physical environment. The baby's deliberate and exhaustive exploration of a novel object is mirrored in the scientist at the microscope or the explorer in unfamiliar territory. The rapt attention of the child drawing in the dirt with a stick or creating a house with play bricks may be seen on the face of the artist or architect. The child's delight in dramatic play and in social rituals or games is reflected in the adult's printed or performed dramas and in the elaborate rules and rituals of cultures. Many adults who find their work rewarding describe it in terms that sound more like play; they enjoy their work so much that they may consider the monetary compensation as simply an additional benefit. Adult play may be more subtle and sophisticated than the play of children, and adults' play materials are likely to be complex machines or abstract concepts rather than "toys." But the basic inclination that leads the child to play remains in the adult. Our minds never stop being active, constructive, and "playful."

Individual and group achievements typically go beyond survival or comfort or coping with the necessities of life. Human achievements suggest the kind of spontaneous exploration and experimentation with the boundaries of reality that is exhibited in play. Play may be one of the most profound expressions of human nature and one of the greatest innate resources for learning and invention. It both expresses and develops our abilities and interests—in complex social interaction, in symbolic representation, in discovering and creating patterns, in mastering skills, and in manipulating, exploring, and controlling the environment. Enlightened support for play, at any age, may be key in helping engage and make use of these tendencies as natural resources and as natural motivation for learning and creative expression.

## Importance of play materials ———————————————

Careful observation of the child at play reveals the arbitrariness of the work/play distinction. The "work" of symbolic representation, exploration, experimentation, mastery, invention, artistic expression, and finding rewarding and appropriate ways of interacting with others is the natural "play" of children. For children, especially, play reflects and supports the process of socialization and the development of thinking (Bretherton 1984; Johnson 1990; Singer & Singer 1990; Smilansky 1990). Play reveals children's interests and nourishes the growing edges of their competence.

Children often "work" on new skills in play and prefer interactions with people and objects at an optimal level of challenge for their abilities.

Young children typically try to play with everything in their environments and with each of their own motor and mental capacities. For instance, as they learn to babble and talk, they

## "Children prefer . . ."

Many of the charts and summaries in this book point out features of play materials that attract children; they describe what children "prefer" in toys. These statements usually come from research in which investigators observe children's choices among objects varying on the dimensions studied. Studies of children's toy preferences are far more plentiful than those on more complex questions, such as how a certain feature affects the quality of children's play or their long-term interest in a toy. Toymakers are understandably interested in what children *choose,* but early childhood professionals want to know more. We want to know what play materials sustain children's interest month in and month out, what materials support children's development and in what ways. The answers to these questions are not as easy to get. Where research is available on quality of play or sustained interest, it is reported. Preference findings are reported because they also matter to teachers and caregivers—if a toy doesn't attract children, they will not play with it at all. But readers should bear in mind that what children prefer, usually studied within a very limited time frame, is not necessarily the same as what is best for their development.

play with sounds and with language. They have many growing edges. The play interests that are supported and encouraged in early childhood may influence the learning skills and conscious learning interests of the future. The information-processing skills developed in activities with people and objects provide a scaffold for continuing development. What the child learns is "fun" can form the foundation for intrinsic motivation now and later. If play is children's natural mode of learning, then appropriate play materials play a significant role in helping to develop their interests, motivation, and social and information-processing skills.

The selection of play materials is therefore very important and involves decisions about the kinds of interests, motivation, and skills we want children to develop. Early childhood education theorists, such as Froebel (1975) and Montessori (1964), thought play materials so important that they developed their own equipment to teach specific concepts through play. Another educator, Caroline Pratt, designed the classic unit blocks as a more open-ended play material for children. There have been debates in the early childhood community about the appropriate mix of "structured" (or closed-ended) and open-ended materials that should be available to children, but both are included in most classrooms (Bredekamp & Rosegrant 1992). Educational theorists and teachers have continued to create play materials to fit their goals and the needs of individual children.

It is important to provide play materials for children that interest them and support the exercise and refinement of their skills. Materials should also have lasting play value and help provide a foundation for future development. Some materials attract brief interest but are soon discarded, and some invite types of play that are not desirable. Teachers and caregivers should give careful attention to selecting and maintaining play materials because, whether we intend it or not, they *do* teach.

The materials we provide or omit shape children's play and send them a message about what we value. The activities suggested and supported by the materials not only lead children into doing and learning certain things, they show children what adults think is desirable or acceptable to do. Our educational and human values are reflected in the range and balance of play materials. For instance, do toys foster social play as well as individual play? Do they encourage both open-ended and "structured" play? To what extent do materials focus on language, artistic expression, construction, numbers, nature, science, society, and so on?

Specific features of the play materials provided are also important. The appearance, construction, and complexity of play materials in relation to children's age, experience, and level of skill may affect their interest, imagination, learning, and safety. Specific features of toys—color, size, details included or effects produced, etc.—have been found to be attractive to children in certain age ranges. Some features may make play items more appropriate for different cultural groups and/or may help to reduce bias. The design and construction of toys, including the materials used, sturdiness, and ease of handling, also influence their play value and safety. The level of complexity and structure in materials also has important effects on children's interest and what they learn.

The way in which materials are maintained and presented also teaches children. If materials are chipped or broken or if pieces are missing, children may learn that materials need not be respected and taken care of. If materials are jumbled together or have no organized space where the child can find and return them, children may learn that the environment is chaotic and unpredictable, and their search for patterns may be hindered or reduced. The selection, presentation, and maintenance of each play material should be considered carefully, because everything teaches and everything matters.

Many children with special needs are included in classrooms with typically developing children. As is the case with all children, play materials should match the developmental age and individual needs of each child. The developmental age of an individual child may exceed or be less than the child's chronological age and may require materials designed for older or younger children. Some children may also require materials that have special adaptations for motor, visual, or auditory disabilities.

Different cultural traditions have provided somewhat different play materials and activities for children in line with their individual expectations for development and beliefs about the world (Bronfenbrenner 1972; Sutton-Smith & Roberts 1981; Sutton-Smith 1992). In this country specific types of materials and activities have been used and recommended by the early childhood community for many decades. In addition, psychological research has provided information on young children's play and play material preferences and how children use different types of materials. This book provides suggestions for play materials for children from birth through age 8, incorporating information from psychological theory and research on play and the overall perspective of the early childhood community on what is developmentally appropriate practice.

## Organization of the book

This book is intended to help people providing education and care for young children to select play materials that are safe, appropriate, and supportive of play and development. Included are suggestions for play materials for six different age ranges in early childhood:

— young infants (birth through 6 months)
— older infants (7 through 12 months)
— young toddlers (1 year old)
— older toddlers (2 years old)
— preschool and kindergarten children (3 through 5 years)
— primary-school children (6 through 8 years)

Each of the following chapters (2 through 7) provides information on play materials for one of these age ranges.

Play materials for children in each of the age ranges are grouped under four general headings, for ease of reference:

— social and fantasy play materials
— exploration and mastery play materials
— music, art, and movement materials
— gross motor play materials

These headings reflect broad categories of play activities that are frequently distinguished and considered important in early childhood education and psychological research. It is important to remember, however, that play materials often support more than one type of play, and children can be engaged in activities that simultaneously support different areas of development. For example, sand and water play frequently involves both exploration of materials and fantasy or social play with others. Similarly, play with blocks may involve both mastery (constructing a road) and dramatic play with others (being race car drivers). Many play materials appropriate for young children support development in a number of areas.

As noted, each of the chapters contains information to assist in the selection of play materials for one of the six age ranges. For each age range this information includes the following:

— abilities and play interests
— initial appropriateness considerations
— suggestions for appropriate materials
— priorities and special considerations

In addition to the information and charts organized by age groups in Chapters 2 through 7, information about play materials by type (puzzles, dolls, musical instruments, etc.) and across age groups is summarized in the "Guide to Play Materials by Type" at the back of the book.

# Selection of age ranges

The choice of age-range divisions was based on a review of developmental research on fine motor, gross motor, social, and cognitive development, and the development of play behavior and play interests in early childhood. The narrower age groupings over the first three years reflect the more rapid developmental changes that occur during the first years of life. The transitions between age groups in the first two years are strongly tied to major motor developments.

### Young infants (birth through 6 months)

During the first six months of life, the infant's attention span and motor control are very limited. Infants respond to interesting sights, sounds, and textures and gradually develop the ability to bat, kick, and grasp objects.

### Older infants (7 through 12 months)

The age break at 7 months is tied to the child's ability to sit unsupported. By 7 months, the child has also developed good grasping abilities and can hold objects in one hand.

### Young toddlers (1 year)

The age break at 1 year reflects the child's rapidly developing mobility. Many children have begun to walk, usually unsteadily, and most are climbing up and down stairs. The child is also beginning to show signs of mental imagery. By about 18 months, the child's language development typically "takes off," and children begin to show symbolic thinking and their first pretend play.

### Older toddlers (2 years)

By age 2, children's large muscle development is sufficient to permit them to explore a wider range of objects and activities and to engage in a lot of gross motor activity. In addition, a growing sense of independence motivates them to test and demonstrate their power. The period between 2 and 3 years is a time when children are moving into the more advanced fantasy and role play of the preschooler, but they are still tied to action and movement, and exploration dominates their activities with objects.

### Preschool and kindergarten children (3 through 5 years)

The period from 3 through 5 years is often treated as a whole and labeled the "preschool years." Although there is considerable motor, cognitive, language, and socioemotional growth and change during this period, the changes do not seem as dramatic or discontinuous as during the previous three years. Five-year-olds are included in the age range, based on the evidence that a major developmental shift occurs in the period between 5 and 7 years (White 1970). Before this shift, children resemble preschoolers more than they resemble school-age children in terms of their socioemotional development and their thinking. Classrooms with vertical grouping sometimes include 5-year-olds with 3- and 4-year-olds and sometimes with 6- and 7-year-olds.

### Primary-school children (6 through 8 years)

A large change occurs at around 6 or 7 years, when the child has been described across cultures as acquiring "sense," that is, responsibility and conscious self-direction (Whiting & Edwards 1988). The primary-school period, which includes ages 6 through 8, marks the end of the early childhood period. Critical developmental changes during this period are both cognitive (at the level of logical and symbolic thinking) and socioemotional. In the developmental literature, the age of 9 marks a time when children's physical skills have become quite mature. Children after this age are typically more capable of reading and following directions and of consciously developing their own plans and strategies.

## Groupings of the play materials

Play materials are grouped into four types of play: social and fantasy; exploration and mastery; music, art, and movement; and gross motor play. Of course, children can and do use almost any play item in various ways in their play. However, to make this handbook manageable to use, we list a material under multiple groupings only when children's typical use of a play item seems to fall more or less equally into more than one grouping. The groupings of the materials according to type of play are as follows:

*Social and fantasy play materials* include materials that nourish the child's growing imagination and encourage mental representation of objects, scenes, events, and processes. Social and fantasy play materials also support the child's growing understanding of people (both self and others) and the roles and rules involved in social interaction. Play materials under this heading may be used in dramatic play, solitary fantasy play, or more structured games with others and include such items as dolls, puppets, role-play materials (props and costume materials for housekeeping, workplace, school, space exploration, etc.), and transportation toys. Simple turn-taking games and early board games are also included here. Construction materials, such as unit blocks and Legos, are included under both "Social and fantasy play materials" and "Exploration and mastery play materials," with their play value under each heading noted. Books are important in almost all aspects of development and are mentioned under a variety of headings for each age range.

*Exploration and mastery play materials* include materials that nourish and extend the child's interest and knowledge about the physical world, support the child's attempts to discover or invent ways to structure and understand it, and introduce the child to linguistic and scientific categories (concepts) that others have discovered/invented to help in understanding the physical world. Also included here are materials that focus on helping the child to develop specific information-processing or problem-solving (learning-to-learn) skills and/or to master specific techniques. The materials are typically used in play that focuses on exploration, experimentation, or goal-oriented mastery and include construction materials; puzzles; pattern-making materials (pegboards, geometric shapes, etc.); dressing, lacing, and stringing materials; sand and water (and other plastic media) materials; and specific skill-development materials (matching, sorting, counting, sound and letter discrimination, etc.). There are also books for children on many of the topics included under this heading.

*Music, art, and movement materials* are designed to support the development of a variety of forms of artistic expression. Materials that foster both participation and appreciation are recommended. Art and craft materials, rhythm and musical instruments, and audiovisual equipment are included, as well as books about relevant topics.

*Gross motor play materials* include those designed to foster large muscle development and skills. Push-and-pull toys; ride-on equipment; and outdoor, gym, and sports equipment are listed here. Some of these are also mentioned under "Social and fantasy play materials."

## Selection criteria for materials

In general, age range should be chosen with several considerations in mind. Appropriate play materials should be

- appealing and interesting to the child;
- appropriate for the child's physical capacities;
- appropriate for the child's mental and social development;
- appropriate for use in groups of children; and
- well constructed, durable, and safe for the ages of the children in the group.

| Initial Considerations | Specific Features |
| --- | --- |
| Size/construction of object | Overall dimensions (weight, ease of handling)<br>Size/number of parts<br>Construction/removability of parts |
| Materials | Type of materials<br>Color/contrast<br>Audio or visual effects |
| Complexity/detail/structure | Perceptual or conceptual complexity<br>Lifelike appearance<br>Level of structure (closed- vs. open-ended) |
| Fine motor skills required | Ease of manipulation<br>Ease of assembly<br>Actions involved |
| Gross motor skills required | Coordination required for operation<br>Coordination required for safety |
| Cognitive development/<br>knowledge required | Interest features for age |
| Safety | Sturdiness/breakability<br>Sharpness of edges/points<br>Size of small parts for choking/swallowing<br>hazard<br>Nontoxicity of materials<br>Appropriateness for gross/fine motor abilities |

The play value of materials—their usefulness in supporting the growth and development of children through play—is the foremost consideration in the selection process. Cost is also an important factor for all programs to varying degrees, and ways of cutting costs are discussed in the recommendations for each age range.

The suggestions in the book are based on (1) a review of the relevant literature on child development, play, and the use of play materials; and (2) analysis of specific characteristics of the materials to determine features that are important in evaluating appropriateness for the age ranges under consideration. The literature on children's play and development suggests that at different ages there are evolving abilities and play interests, so these are briefly outlined for each age range. *It is important to remember, however, that the needs, interests, and abilities of the children served in a program may differ from those of children in other groups, so the baseline for selecting materials should always be the children themselves.*

The literature also suggests that certain features of play materials may be particularly important for children's development, safety, or interest at specific ages. These features are grouped under seven categories, which are called "Initial appropriateness considerations" because they affect the basic suitability of play materials. Materials were evaluated according to these considerations—and for their play value in a group setting—before being included in the recommendations. The opinions of experts and findings from psychological research were also used in establishing the seven initial considerations for evaluating the appropriateness of play materials for an age group. The initial appropriateness considerations are listed in the table on page 9, with the specific features used in making judgments.

In looking at the appropriateness of specific toys for an early childhood program, each of these features should be considered with respect to the children the program will serve. Guidelines can only be approximate because the range of individual differences may be great. A fuller description of the criteria used for evaluating toys is presented below to assist early childhood professionals in making their own judgments.

In looking at the *size and construction* of play materials, three aspects are evaluated:

- *overall dimensions* (weight, volume, length, width, and height), especially as these affect the object's ease of handling for children of a given age;
- *number and size of parts,* considered in relation to the manipulative skills, cognitive abilities, and preferences that characterize children of a given age;
- *construction* of the object, for instance, whether parts are removable, edges are rounded, or the object as a whole is stable (i.e., not easily tipped).

Although research often provides broad guidelines for toy size and design, it rarely indicates the precise dimensions that a toy should be for children of a given age. In selecting equipment and play materials, staff need to think in terms of the size and motor development of the children in the program.

Evaluation in terms of *materials* means considering qualities of the play item such as

- the *substance* from which it is made: hardness/softness, washability, breakability, heaviness);
- *color,* as it pertains to educational value and children's preferences; and
- *special effects* included—audio (sounds, music, words) or visual (lights, movements)—with respect to age appropriateness and chil-

dren's preferences. The needs and interests of the group of children served provide further definition for this criterion. The play materials appropriate for children may vary with individual or cultural differences or other local factors, such as climate.

Toys vary with respect to perceptual or conceptual *complexity,* the degree of realistic *detail* or representational qualities, and closed- or open-ended *structure.* Children's development is a major determinant of the appropriate level of complexity or detail in their play objects. For instance, a 2-year-old needs a simpler, less detailed puzzle than a 5-year-old. There is play value in both open-ended play materials (e.g., blocks, clay, sand, paint) for the child to organize and structure and closed-ended materials (e.g., puzzles, nesting boxes, matching cards) for which the child needs to discover the structure. Although the needs of the children served determine appropriateness, characteristics of play materials are somewhat relative to children's culture and experiences. Play materials can address these differences if they have features that are culturally familiar and that help children grow in their understanding of others.

Determining the *fine motor skills needed* to use a play material requires consideration of several characteristics:

- *actions* required (twisting, snapping, etc.);
- *fine motor skills* needed to perform these actions;
- *strength* required for manipulation or assembly; and
- *number of sequenced or complex actions* necessary.

Of course, the needs and abilities of the children served are of primary concern.

An evaluation of the *gross motor skills required* to use an object or material requires an estimate of the large muscle *coordination* needed for rewarding, safe use and defines age appropriateness in terms of the age at which children commonly develop the skills needed to operate materials of that type. Because a specific age group may include children with a wide range of gross motor skills, the children served in a program always provide the ultimate criterion to use in judging appropriateness.

It is also necessary to consider the *knowledge required* to use an object or play material appropriately and safely. This evaluation involves thinking about what kinds of cognitive and social knowledge and reasoning ability the child needs to play with the material and what knowledge can be expected of children at different ages. Because background knowledge and expectations are related to children's culture and experiences, many factors about the group of children being served enter into decisions about appropriate materials when considering the knowledge required to use them.

A major area of consideration for all play materials is their durability and *safety* when being handled by a number of children over time. Materials for early childhood programs should be constructed to withstand the uses and abuses of children in the age range for which they are appropriate.

# What the Government Requires

Mandatory Toy Safety Regulations

## For All Ages

- Electrical toys must present no shock or thermal hazards.
- The amount of lead in toy paint is extremely limited.
- Toys must contain no toxic materials.

### *Providers of early education and care can also*

- examine age and safety labels on materials.
- explain and/or show children how to use materials properly and safely.
- keep materials intended for older children away from younger children who can be injured.
- check all materials periodically for breakage and potential hazards—damaged or dangerous materials should be repaired or thrown away immediately.
- store materials safely; teach children to put away materials so that they do not become tripping hazards, and check boxes and shelves for safety.
- understand that some materials that are safe for individual children may not be safe for use in groups; take group use and supervision requirements into account when selecting materials.

## For Children Younger than Age 3

- Materials should be unbreakable—able to withstand use and abuse.
- No play material should contain small parts or pieces that could become lodged in the throat.

# What the Toy Industry Does

Voluntary Standards for Toy Safety

- puts age and safety labels on toys*
- puts warning labels on crib gyms advising that they be removed from the crib when babies can get up on hands and knees (to prevent strangling)
- makes squeeze toys and teethers large enough so as not to become lodged in an infant's throat
- makes strings on crib and playpen toys no longer than 12 inches so that the cords cannot become wrapped around children's necks

• Infant manipulables should be large enough to not become lodged in the throat and constructed so as to not separate into small pieces.

*Providers of early education and care can also*
• regularly check materials for cleanliness, sharp edges, points, splinters, peeling paint, etc.
• see that materials are safe for mouthing and are able to be thoroughly washed.
• select soft toys (for infants and toddlers) that are made of non-fuzzy materials (avoid velour and terry cloth) and can be thoroughly washed.
• avoid foam play materials for infants and toddlers because pieces can be chewed off and swallowed and present a choking hazard.
• make certain that mobiles and visuals for infants are suspended with safety in mind and are out of reach if not designed for manipulation.
• avoid attaching grasping materials for infants to the sides of cribs with ribbons, strings, elastic, etc., because infants or their clothing can become entangled, resulting in the infant being strangled.

## For Children Younger than Age 8
• No electrically operated toys should contain heating elements.
• Toys should have no sharp points.
• Toys should have no sharp edges.

The Consumer Product Safety Commission can also remove materials from the marketplace that present hazards not covered by the above regulations.

• installs mechanisms in toy chests to ensure that the lid will stay open in any position to which it is raised and not fall unexpectedly on a child

For further information about these issues, write to the *U.S. Consumer Product Safety Commission*, Washington, DC 20207, or call the toll-free hotline, 1-800-638-CPSC.

---

*Note that the focus of these labels is on safety rather than appropriateness. Industry age labeling cannot be relied upon for guidance about the usefulness of a toy for a specific age.

Play materials should also be regularly inspected for damage and carefully maintained to ensure that they remain safe.

The U.S. Consumer Product Safety Commission (CPSC) has set safety regulations for certain play materials. Manufacturers must design and construct their products to meet these regulations to prevent the sale of hazardous products. In addition, many toy manufacturers adhere to the toy industry's voluntary safety standards.

# Chapter 2

# Young Infants
# (birth through 6 months)

# Abilities and play interests

An overview of typical abilities and play interests of young infants from birth through 6 months—in the motor, perceptual-cognitive, and social-linguistic domains—is outlined below to provide a background for considering appropriate play materials. Not all children will fit these average patterns or demonstrate all of these abilities and interests. From the beginning, children show a range of individual differences that provide a further filter and framework for the selection and use of play materials.

## *Motor*

- makes movements more smoothly and more purposefully
- gains control of hands—learns to bat, then reach and grasp objects (with entire hand)
- discovers feet—brings feet to mouth and explores with feet
- begins to sit with support and can play in a supported sitting position
- engages in large muscle play, including rolling, scooting, rocking, and bouncing

## *Perceptual-cognitive*

- follows objects with eyes, as visual focus matures; continues to gaze in direction of moving objects that disappear, but does not search for an object hidden from view
- learns to localize sounds and turns to see
- responds to rhythm, music, singing (may move, jiggle, or make sounds)
- develops visually directed reaching
- explores the world with eyes and ears and begins to explore with hands, feet, and mouth
- enjoys creating effects in the environment by own actions
- begins to recognize familiar people, objects, and events, then to anticipate them
- becomes aware of novelty and strangeness in people, objects, and events

- may imitate simple movements if they are in own repertoire
- does one thing at a time

## *Social-linguistic*

- shows special interest in people (faces and voices especially)
- begins to smile at faces, voices, and mirror image
- becomes quiet upon visual or voice contact with people
- begins to seek attention and contact with people
- vocalizes in response to social contact and sounds produced by others
- reacts differentially to emotional tone of others' voices (angry vs. friendly)
- distinguishes among familiar people and has preferences
- begins to coo and gurgle, babble, and laugh aloud; plays with sounds
- listens to voices and may imitate sounds already in own repertoire

# Initial appropriateness considerations _____

Play materials for young infants are primarily for looking, listening, sucking, grasping, or fingering. Even before they can effectively bat or grasp objects, infants enjoy seeing and hearing interesting things. Infants like to see

- bright, primary colors;
- high contrast;
- simple design;
- clear lines and features;
- human facial features (especially eyes); and
- bull's-eye pattern.

They enjoy watching hanging objects or mobiles that are moved by wind, wind-up action, or their own activity. From the earliest ages infants enjoy producing predictable or mildly novel effects by their own activity. Materials for watching are more appealing if they move and make noise, but movement should be slow and noises not too loud or sudden.

Infants enjoy variety within a generally predictable environment. They are learning to distinguish features and regularities in the environment and are discovering their own ability to affect what happens in it. As with older children (and even adults), preference for novelty versus familiarity and predictability differs from child to child. Materials and activities that delight some may overwhelm or frighten others. Repetition that pleases some babies may bore others. It is useful to adopt an experimental attitude and carefully monitor individual children's responses to different materials, activities, and levels of novelty or stimulation.

Infants need to experience the social and material world as safe, providing for their biological needs, reasonably predictable, interesting, and responsive. During the first six months, play materials should support children's beginning efforts to explore the environment, discover pattern and regularity in it, and produce desired or interesting effects through their own efforts. Not all materials suggested in the following sections will interest or engage all infants, because even newborns demonstrate a considerable range of individual differences and preferences.

YOUNG INFANTS

## Suggestions for appropriate materials ⎯⎯⎯⎯⎯⎯

Even in the early months of life, infants are experiencing their physical and social environment. Long before they can move around, they explore with their eyes, attend to sounds, and manipulate objects within their grasp. Already there are many materials that support their development.

### *Social and fantasy play materials*

Although young infants are not yet engaging in true social or fantasy play, they enjoy toys that are later used in such play, and they show an interest in "social features," such as faces and voices.

#### Mirrors

Crib mirrors (shown on p. 20) and infant wall mirrors (shown on p. 43) encourage self-awareness, and infants as young as 2 months of age enjoy them. Babies smile at their mirror images by the third month. Infants are fascinated by faces and are much amused by their own faces, although they might not recognize the image as their own face until about 6 months. For safety, mirrors for young infants should be unbreakable and have no sharp edges. They should be firmly mounted —perhaps on the side of a crib or over a changing area—at a convenient height for infant viewing. For optimal support in developing self-awareness, mirrors should be large enough for infants to see their faces and their body movements. Infants spontaneously discover many of the interesting features of mirrors, but adults can also bring some features into awareness by making interesting reflected gestures and actions with play materials. The adult can bring a hand close to a mirror, making interesting finger movements or holding a toy to attract the infant's attention, then move it toward the infant or back and forth from the mirror.

## Dolls

Infants use soft or rag dolls as grasping toys. Dolls for infants should be soft all over, lightweight, and simple in design. This simplicity includes simple facial characteristics (painted or molded hair, no movable eyes, features sewn or painted on), and simple, one-piece bodies (with no movable limbs). The dolls should have no accessories or detachable parts or clothes. They should be able to be easily grasped and explored by the child and be approximately 8 to 13 inches in length. Faces in general and eyes in particular are important to infants, and they prefer brightly colored or patterned materials. Facial features should contrast sharply so that they stand out. Schematic and brightly colored dolls are more appropriate for this age group than are ethnically representative or realistic figures. Dolls that have rattles inside or that make some kind of noise when shaken are interesting for this age group because the infants can produce effects by moving the dolls.

Dolls for infants should be completely washable and should always be washed before being used by another child. Although not necessary in group settings, soft dolls and other soft objects appeal to infants and may soothe and reassure them. Some children become attached to particular soft, cuddly toys at home (dolls, stuffed animals) and are comforted by having these with them when away from home. Objects brought from home to comfort a child should not be used by other infants.

## Stuffed toys/play animals

Young infants use small plush animals (8 to 12 inches long) and grab-on soft toys for grasping, mouthing, and exploring. As with dolls, infants prefer stuffed animals with bright colors and strongly contrasting facial

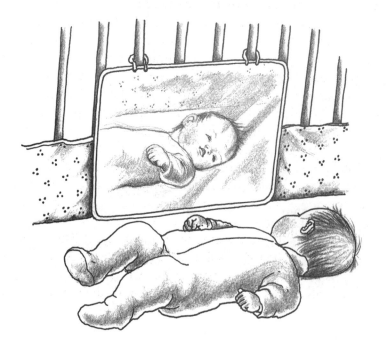

features. Eyes and noses on animals should be permanently attached (sewn or painted), and there should be no whiskers, ribbons, bells, or buttons. Stuffed animals for infants should not be furry, and they should be completely washable. Babies enjoy stuffed toys with rattles or bells inside because they produce interesting effects when shaken. Although stuffed animals are difficult to keep clean and are not necessary in group settings, infants are attracted to them and may benefit from their soothing presence. As in the case of dolls, some children become attached to specific stuffed toys at home and are comforted by their presence when away from home. Again, objects brought from home should not be used by other infants.

YOUNG INFANTS

### Puppets

Although true puppet play does not appear until the preschool period, even young infants may respond to soft hand puppets held and moved by other people. Adults or older children can increase the baby's interest by accompanying the movements with special sounds, words, or songs.

## *Exploration and mastery play materials*

Although young infants are primarily exploring objects and their own developing fine motor skills, they enjoy producing interesting effects and learn to do this deliberately.

### Mobiles/visuals

Mobiles and visual displays for infants are designed primarily for the first six months of life. These objects allow infants to explore with their eyes and help them to focus on and follow objects visually. Most materials in this category are intended to be visual only, but they encourage reaching, and some are designed so that the infant can bang, kick, or shake them by his own movements. A few are designed for later use as grasping toys. When children begin to be able to reach and grasp objects (typically, at 4 to 6 months), they are less interested in things that cannot be touched and manipulated. Any objects that cannot be safely handled by infants *must be raised out of reach* at this point, and each child should be carefully monitored, because the abilities to reach and grasp may develop at different times.

Mobiles and visuals should not be more than 14 inches from the eyes for infants younger than 3 months, then gradually raised higher as children's focus improves. The size of the object should not be greater than can be accommodated within the visual field (about 6 to 18 inches across for mobiles, depending on the distance from the eyes). The displays should be oriented toward the infant's line of sight and designed so that the interesting sights and effects are clearly visible when the baby is lying on her back. Infants in this age range prefer a few, distinct features rather than many, complex features. They also prefer patterned, over plain-color, stimuli; they are attentive to clear edges, accentuated features and pattern markers, and faces—especially the eyes. Infants also prefer moving rather than static displays, and they like displays accompanied by sound. The movement should not be too fast or too slow or infants will not be able to follow it visually, and sudden movements could startle them. Infants prefer rhythmic sounds and do not like sudden or loud sounds. Infants also may enjoy variety, so displays can be changed or modified when a child's interest begins to decline.

Mobiles and visuals may interest infants for relatively long periods of time, especially if the infants can exert some control over the effects they perceive. Infants need contact with people, as well, and it is important that these (or any other) materials not be used as substitutes for appropriate social interaction with adults.

## Grasping toys

Grasping toys are for simple hand manipulation and mouthing and become appropriate at about 3 months of age, when the infant begins to hold and explore objects. Grasping toys help to develop visually directed reaching and eye–hand coordination, as well as to encourage the child to try out and practice fine motor skills. They allow the infant to produce interesting effects by his own action and experience being a cause in simple cause-and-effect relationships. Rattles, teethers, squeeze toys, and light, graspable cloth toys are appropriate as the first grasping materials. Sound and visual effects resulting from the infant's batting and grasping efforts add to a toy's appeal. The adult can hold objects near or touching an infant's hand to encourage the first grasping efforts. Infants gradually learn to reach for objects and gradually gain accuracy in reaching.

The 4- to 6-month-old infant may reach for and grasp objects, bring them to her mouth, and do some simple manipulations, such as shaking and squeezing. She begins to engage in object play and be actively interested in creating effects. Providing a variety of objects to support and encourage exploration is desirable. Although the infant may play with only one object at a time, providing for choice and comparison among several objects is useful, and the child may develop favorites.

Infants in this age group continue to enjoy rattles, teethers, and simple cloth toys. They also like other, slightly more complex hand-held manipulables: nipple balls, plastic disks on a ring, grasping balls, and interlocking plastic rings (a few). When babies begin to sit up, they enjoy toys on suction cups that are attached to the table or tray in front of them. The suction cups keep the play materials relatively stable and in sight so that children can explore the objects' properties and clearly see specific effects produced by their actions on the objects.

Grasping toys for this age group should be lightweight; have bright, primary colors; and be able to be easily grasped from any angle. The taste, texture, and smell of the objects add interest. Grasping toys should be simple in design and require only simple manipulations (shaking, squeezing) to create effects.

YOUNG INFANTS

## Music, art, and movement materials

Although young infants cannot play musical instruments, they enjoy producing interesting sounds with bells and rattles, and they respond to music from birth.

### Musical instruments

Although not always recognized as such, the rattles and bells enjoyed by infants are simple rhythm instruments (and are used as such by older children). Young infants kick, bat, or shake rhythm materials to produce interesting sounds rather than to make music. Children play with sound, including their own voices, almost from birth. The sounds produced by the play materials should be clear but not so loud as to startle the child. Small bells with handles, infant wrist bells for the hand or foot, and rattles of various kinds are appropriate for this age group. For safety, these materials should be light, unbreakable, and have no removable parts, sharp edges, or points. Like all play materials for this age, these objects should be washable.

### Audiovisual materials

Infants, from the earliest ages, enjoy rhythms, music, and singing. They especially enjoy and are soothed by gentle, repeated rhythms ("heartbeat" rhythms from birth through 2 months, presumably because these sounds were familiar before birth), soothing lullabies, simple songs, and soft, gentle tunes. Babies like repeated words or sounds and musical themes, because they are learning to discriminate audio patterns. They react to changes in volume and may be distressed by loud or sudden recorded noises, just as they are by such sounds in their environment. At 3 to 6 months infants can localize sounds, begin to babble, and make singing sounds with an adult.

Appropriate audiovisual equipment for this age range includes music boxes (wound by adults, of course) and records/tapes/compact discs with appropriate rhythms, tunes, and songs.

## Gross motor play materials

Although young infants may move their whole bodies in reaction to interesting sights or sounds, gross motor play materials are not relevant to

| Overview of Play Materials for Young Infants— | |
| --- | --- |
| **Social and Fantasy<br>Play Materials** | **Exploration and Mastery<br>Play Materials** |
| **Mirrors**<br>well-secured crib and wall mirrors<br>(rounded edges; unbreakable)<br>**Dolls**<br>soft-bodied or rag dolls (lightweight;<br>painted; stitched or molded hair and<br>features; faces and eyes of focal interest)<br>**Stuffed toys/play animals**<br>washable soft animals (simple in design;<br>bright colors; contrasting features that are<br>painted, stitched, or molded)<br>**Puppets**<br>simple hand puppets (for holding and<br>moving by adults—of visual and social<br>interest) | **Mobiles/visuals**<br>hung materials that move slowly and gently<br>for visual focus and tracking (angled toward<br>infants' eyes; hung at appropriate distance;<br>simple in design with high contrast;<br>movement may be accompanied by gentle<br>sounds; TO BE KEPT OUT OF REACH)<br>**Grasping toys**<br>(from about 6 to 8 weeks)<br>simple rattles<br>teethers<br>squeeze toys<br>light, sturdy cloth toys<br>(from about 4 months)<br>disks, keys on ring<br>interlocking rings (few)<br>grasping/nipple balls<br>small hand-held manipulables<br>toys on suction cups (when child is able to sit) |

this age group. As soon as they can grasp, many infants enjoy clutch and texture balls, but these items are explored as grasping toys rather than used as gross motor play materials.

Crib and play gyms are materials suspended over the child for swiping, batting, grasping, or kicking. They are interesting to children from about 3 months of age, but there are safety issues connected with their use. Those models spanning cribs should be firmly attached, but they should be removed when the child can push up on hands and knees (or they become strangling hazards). Newer models have a freestanding structure and can be used on the floor. Children at these early ages use these materials for batting and grasping rather than for gross motor play. Infants may reach and grasp, shake and pull, and enjoy creating interesting effects. Gyms for this age range should be simple in design—simple enough for the child to understand what effects she is producing and how she is producing them. The parts designed for manipulation should be light and easy for a child of this age range to manipulate, but the objects should also be unbreakable. All parts should have rounded edges and be washable. As with other materials for this age group, bright, primary colors with high contrast are recommended. The sound and/or visual effects produced by the child's activity should be clear but not too loud, sudden, or extreme, as this might frighten the child.

## Birth through 6 Months

| Music, Art, and Movement Play Materials | Gross Motor Play Materials |
| --- | --- |
| **Musical instruments** (from about 6 to 8 weeks) bell on handle wrist/ankle bells rattles **Audiovisual materials** adult-operated music boxes records, tapes, CDs, etc. with gentle, regular rhythms, songs, lullabies | **Large-movement materials** balls—clutch and texture (precursors to later gross motor play) crib and play gyms (used with supervision and special attention to safety; simple in design with clear but gentle effects produced by action of hands or feet) |

Although the four categories provide a useful classification, play materials can typically be used in more than one way and could be listed under more than one of the categories.

## Priorities and special considerations

**Priorities** for play materials for infants from birth through 6 months old include

1. a range of interesting things to see, hear, and touch;
2. materials that support the infant's developing self-awareness;
3. materials that allow the infant to produce effects;
4. materials that are safe.

From objects or events that are entirely familiar to those that are highly novel, the point on the continuum that is most interesting and enjoyable is not the same for all children. Moreover, preferences vary for the same child on different occasions and at different points in development. A range of options to try out should be available as the child develops, but a few objects at a time are enough; these can be rotated to maintain interest.

Mirrors support the development of self-awareness. Infants a few months old enjoy visuals or grasping toys that allow them to produce effects, and these materials promote infants' interest in exploration. Safely suspended objects to bat, kick, or (later) grasp, especially those that respond with movement or (gentle) noise, are examples of such items.

### Infants birth through 6 months

Basic play materials for young infants:

❑ unbreakable mirrors that can be attached to a crib, changing table, or other play area

❑ one or two special items, such as dolls and stuffed animals, that may be brought from home as comfort items for individual children (for hygienic reasons, not to be used by other infants)

❑ a variety of mobiles/visuals that can be changed and rotated among infants

❑ a variety of toys that infants can bat or kick, mouth, grasp, and manipulate

❑ rattles and bells (with a handle or for the wrist or ankle) that make interesting sounds when manipulated

Although appropriate play materials can support and promote development, other people are of primary importance in the infant's world. Adults and other children are very interesting to infants, and interaction with adults is especially important. Infants are soothed by the presence of an adult and pay special attention to the faces and voices of familiar adults. As their vision matures infants enjoy watching the activities of older children (from a safe vantage point) if the noise is not loud and the movements are not too fast for them to follow.

Safety is a primary consideration in selecting play materials for all children, but materials for infants and children younger than 3 must meet especially rigorous requirements. Because children's needs and capacities differ, staff must always consider whether toys are safe for the children served and for use by those children under the conditions existing in the care environment (considering numbers of children, amount of individual attention available, etc.). Children's developing capacities should also be carefully monitored, because a toy that has been safe for a child may become hazardous almost overnight as the child acquires a new skill or capacity. For instance, a low-hanging mobile that has been safe for a child who cannot reach and grasp must be moved when the child's capacities improve unless the mobile is designed to meet the safety requirements for grasping toys. Crib gyms are safe for children lying on their backs but become hazardous when children can get onto hands and knees, because they can become entangled in and even strangled by the gyms.

**Special considerations** in group care for young infants include *cost, children's health,* and *safety.* Many mobiles and visuals for infants may be handmade from inexpensive materials, such as heavy paper or cardboard. Because infants do not touch mobiles, sturdy construction is not necessary, but the items must be mounted securely and out of reach. Simple grasping toys can also be made, but safe materials and construction must be a primary consideration. Household and recycled items can be used to make interesting grasping toys if they meet the stringent safety criteria for the age group.

Health is a major concern in the care of infants and must always be considered in the purchase and care of materials. Look for materials that can be regularly and thoroughly washed and disinfected. When materials cannot be completely washed and disinfected before being used by each child (as in the case of cloth and stuffed toys), each child should have her or his own individual materials.

YOUNG INFANTS

# Chapter 3

# Older Infants
# (7 through 12 months)

## Abilities and play interests _____

An overview of typical abilities and play interests of older infants from 7 through 12 months—in the motor, perceptual-cognitive, and social-linguistic domains—is outlined below to provide a background for considering appropriate play materials. As with any age group, not all infants of 7 through 12 months fit these average patterns or demonstrate all of the abilities and interests mentioned. Because children always show a range of individual differences, the specific characteristics of children in the program are always primary considerations when selecting play materials and planning for their use.

### *Motor*

- begins to sit alone
- begins to creep and crawl onto or into things
- begins to pull to a stand, cruise (walk while holding furniture), and walk alone (10–16 months)
- shows interest in moving about and practicing motor skills
- develops "pincer" (thumb and finger) grasp and begins to hold objects with one hand while manipulating them with the other
- begins to transfer objects from one hand to the other
- begins to stack objects
- wants to bang, insert, poke, twist, squeeze, drop, shake, bite, throw, open/shut, push/pull, empty/fill, drag along objects
- enjoys bath play—kicking and splashing

### *Perceptual-cognitive*

- shows interest in appearing and disappearing objects and people—develops object permanence (at approximately 11 months, looks for object out of sight)
- shows interest in container/contained relationship—likes to empty cupboards, drawers, and containers of objects
- enjoys letting go and dropping objects (uses string to pull back objects that have been dropped over the edge of a play table or highchair)

- enjoys exploring items and likes many objects to explore
- likes to operate simple mechanisms (open/shut, push/pull) and create effects
- shows persistence and interest in novelty
- remembers people, objects, games, actions with toys
- begins to search for hidden object (at approximately 11 months)
- begins to show interest in picture books

## *Social-linguistic*

- may fear strangers or react badly to change; plays best with familiar person nearby
- watches and sometimes imitates others
- shows awareness of social approval and disapproval
- enjoys getting attention and creating social effects
- enjoys simple social games, such as peekaboo and bye-bye
- babbles and plays with language—may try to imitate sounds
- enjoys songs and may vocalize and move to music/rhythm
- recognizes own name and may begin to point to named objects or obey simple commands

## Initial appropriateness considerations _____

Infants in this age range engage in longer periods of active exploration of objects. As their motor capacities improve, older infants like to perform many different exploratory activities. A range of play materials that provide opportunities to practice and expand skills are useful and enjoyed. Toward the end of the first year, infants begin to show interest in mastering simple operations with objects. Play materials can support this interest by presenting simple challenges, such as stacking, filling and emptying, and fitting one object into another. Older infants also enjoy operating simple mechanisms and producing effects by their own actions.

As the large motor capacities of older infants develop, their play may involve creeping, crawling, pulling to a stand, and, sometimes, beginning to stand alone or walk. Materials that facilitate these activities are helpful and interesting to children. As they become more mobile, older infants also try to obtain objects beyond their immediate reach. They are challenged by having some play materials placed a short distance away and use their developing motor skills to reach them.

Older infants are interested in social contact and gaining attention from adults through their own activities. They learn from watching others and may try to imitate many simple actions, sounds, or activities with objects they see. Appropriate modeling, adult responsiveness, and interaction with older infants during daily care routines and some of their play episodes can support social and language development and enhance object play. Adults can support the child's interest in social interaction and communication by initiating and responding to communication efforts, modeling simple repetitive verbal or action games and routines, and providing verbal labels for play objects, events, and the child's own activities. In addition to being interesting for solitary exploration and mastery, many play materials can provide springboards for interaction.

**OLDER INFANTS**

## Suggestions for appropriate materials _____

With their rapid motor and intellectual development during the first year of life, infants 6 to 12 months old are able to enjoy a wider variety of play materials, which support their social, cognitive, and physical development.

### *Social and fantasy play materials*

Many of the social and fantasy play materials that are appropriate for younger infants are still appropriate for older infants—with more emphasis on their manipulability.

#### Mirrors

Mirrors help older infants develop awareness of themselves and their movements in space. When children can sit up, smaller mirrors that can be held and manipulated become suitable. Large, low, wall-mounted mirrors (shown on p. 43) enable infants to see themselves sit, crawl, and begin to walk. All hand and wall mirrors must be unbreakable, sturdy enough to withstand being bumped, and have no sharp edges, and wall mirrors should be firmly mounted. Clarity of image is important so that children can observe themselves and their actions without distortion.

#### Dolls

The soft, simple dolls appropriate for young infants (see p. 20) are also suitable for older infants, who still use the dolls primarily as grasping toys.

#### Puppets

Although true puppet play does not appear until the preschool period, older infants respond to a puppet held and moved by an adult. They may want to handle and explore the puppet, so the materials should be sturdy and washable.

### Stuffed toys/play animals

The small plush animals (8 to 12 inches) appropriate for young infants (see pp. 20–21) are also appropriate for older infants. In addition, mobile infants enjoy, and are comforted by, very large soft toys for hugging, tumbling, and cuddling against. Soft rubber or vinyl animals (6 to 8 inches in height or length) may be explored by older infants and are useful for language development as adults repeat their names.

### Transportation toys

Infants who can sit and move may enjoy simple, one-piece cars for grasping and pushing along the floor. They should be relatively light (so they can be lifted easily) but sturdy and should have large wheels or rollers. They need very little detail because children do not recognize their representational qualities until the end of the first year. For safety, there should be no small windows that could trap children's fingers and no small parts or sharp edges. They should have a rounded, molded appearance. The optimal size of vehicles for this age is 6 to 8 inches. Children typically prefer cars that are brightly colored and those that make noise when pushed.

## Exploration and mastery play materials

When infants are able to sit up and begin to manipulate objects with their hands, a number of play materials become appropriate.

### Grasping toys

During the latter half of the first year, when older infants can sit alone, their hands are free for more complex manipulation and experimentation. By the end of this period, many can crawl or creep to reach objects. They explore and experiment, seeing what can be done with objects and using them as simple tools. They can obtain an object, transfer it from one hand to another, and hold two objects at once. They may use two hands and all 10 fingers in their explorations. They pull, push, crumple, squeeze, rub, slide, poke, twist, shape, and fold objects. Infants in this age range begin to match their exploratory activities (pushing, twisting, squeezing) to the different characteristics of objects and may get bored with repetition of the same activities.

In addition to materials they previously enjoyed (see pp. 22–23), older infants can play with roly-poly toys; objects in containers; rubber, wood, or plastic beads on rings; large rubber or plastic pop beads (shown on p. 54); key rings; balls with special effects (particularly for creepers and crawlers); and objects that open and shut or appear and disappear (such as pop-up or "surprise" boxes). Older infants are less interested in simple rattles and toys on suction cups. Children at this age drop objects and look after them and release and retrieve objects; they are even able to pull a string to retrieve an object. They put things in and dump them out of containers and are particularly interested in pushing balls and small objects. Toward the end of this period, the infant may become interested in appearing and disappearing objects and begin to retrieve objects that are out of sight.

The infant now enjoys having a larger selection and variety of grasping toys. The complexity of the materials and the motor control required to operate them should gradually evolve to challenge the infant's growing capacities (although a few favorites may remain attractive). Objects may be put away for a while and then reintroduced for variety and interest.

## Sand and water play materials

After the child develops the ability to sit unsupported, materials for tub and water play become appropriate. The first water toys should be simple floating objects, either shapes or more representational objects such as boats. What the object represents is less important at this age, and the objects need not be detailed, but infants do prefer brightly colored materials and ones that make noise when squeezed or banged. Because infants are not skilled at manipulation, their water play materials should be constructed to float well and to right themselves if turned over in the water.

Sand play materials are not usually recommended for infants, because children at this age cannot be expected to work with sand effectively or handle it safely.

## Construction materials

Because infants in the first year of life are just developing eye–hand coordination and the ability to relate one object to another, they are not yet ready to do actual construction. For infants 7 through 12 months, who can sit up and grasp objects, a set of soft blocks, which can be stacked or used as grasping toys, support developing skills. Infant blocks should be lightweight and made of soft, easily washed materials (cloth, hollow plastic, vinyl), and squeezable blocks are usually recommended for first blocks. Hardwood blocks are too heavy and sharp edged for infants, but from about 9 months, children may begin to successfully manipulate lightweight wood cubes with rounded edges. Unlike the large assortment of blocks of various shapes and sizes that lend themselves to construction, blocks for infants are typically cubes, which are good for stacking. They should be large enough to be easily grasped and carried (2 to 5 inches on a side, depending on the material). Infants are attracted to brightly colored blocks or cloth blocks with simple, high-contrast pictures of familiar objects or animals. Infants will play with only a few blocks (3 or 4) at a time.

## Puzzles

When infants can sit up and manipulate objects with two hands (around 6 to 7 months), simple two- or three-piece fit-together objects are used as grasping toys. They are used to explore and manipulate, rather than as puzzles to be fitted together as a whole. These early puzzles are really prepuzzles that help the infant develop eye–hand coordination and learn the concept of fitting together. The objects should be unbreakable and cleanable and have rounded edges. Infants usually prefer bright colors and contrasts.

### Specific skill-development materials

A variety of play materials may be used to help older infants increase and refine sensory perception and discrimination and to support their developing fine motor skills. Examples of these types of play materials are simple ring-stacking cones; easily nested cups; and activity centers, busy boxes, and pop-up boxes (shown on p. 56).

Some activity centers are designed to be attached to cribs, bathtubs, or other furniture, and some are free-standing boxes or cubes. These objects and pop-up boxes provide opportunities for the older infant to master simple skills, such as opening and closing small doors and pushing buttons to create effects. Most children younger than 1 year can manage only simple motor actions; they are usually not yet capable of more complex manipulations involving dials, switches, or knobs. Activity and pop-up boxes designed for this age group must be easy to manipulate, because stiff, hard-to-move doors and dials can be frustrating. Any pop-up action in materials should not be too sudden because it might frighten some infants. For safety reasons, adult supervision is recommended when infants handle play materials that spring back quickly or with some force after being pushed down.

Texture pads or blankets (shown below) made of a variety of materials, which provide different sensations to the child sitting or crawling on the blanket, are suitable for older infants and may help their developing awareness of texture differences. Texture pads are most interesting to children who are beginning to creep or crawl, who can explore all the surfaces.

Simple ring-stacking cones with 3 to 5 rings, simple sets of 3 to 5 nesting cups and open containers that may be filled with objects and then emptied support perceptual and fine motor development. All parts of

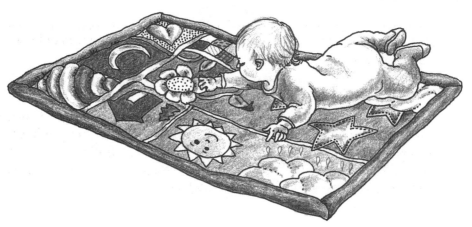

these materials should be light and easily graspable. They should slip into place easily and require no special fitting action. They may be brightly colored, but decoration should be kept to a miminum so that it does not interfere with the child's perception of the concept being presented. For safety, all parts of these materials should be unbreakable, washable, too large to swallow, and have rounded edges. Stacking cones should have a thick, rounded top.

**OLDER INFANTS**

### Books

There are two types of books suitable for infants: books to be handled by the child, and books to be read to the child by an adult.

Books to be handled by infants should be small (no larger than 6 to 8 inches in any direction) and light but sturdy and washable, with few and easily turned pages. The pictures should be simple and clear, with bright colors and high contrast. They should represent familiar objects, animals, or people and have only one or a few objects on a single page. Books for infants usually have only four or five pages. Cloth and light plastic books are suitable for children 6 months and older. There is some debate about whether stiff cardboard books are appropriate for infants younger than 12 months because they tend to be heavy and unwieldy.

Infants may begin to look at pictures in books during the second half of the first year. This period is a good time to begin "lap reading," with the adult showing pictures in books to the infant and talking about what is pictured. Talking about pictures usually generates more interest than reading stories to infants in this age range, but they also enjoy word-for-word reproduction of some rhythmic or rhyming material. Books suitable for adult reading aloud to older infants include the cloth, plastic, or cardboard books handled by the children, other picture books, and nursery rhyme books. The size and construction of books for lap reading need not conform to the standards for books to be handled by infants alone, because the adult holds the book, can turn more fragile pages, and can protect the child and the book from harm.

## *Music, art, and movement materials*

As infants' fine motor skills develop and their interest in exploring expands, they may enjoy making marks on paper and experimenting with different "musical" sounds.

### Art and craft materials

By about 9 to 12 months, some infants are able to hold a crayon to make marks and may scribble. A few large, nontoxic crayons in bright, primary colors may be provided for the child at this point, but real interest in scribbling usually comes after 12 months. Large sheets of paper can be taped to a flat surface to hold them in place for marking.

### Musical instruments

In addition to enjoying the sound-making materials that can be used effectively by younger infants (see p. 23), older infants can successfully use rubber or wood blocks that rattle or tinkle when shaken, banged, or squeezed. For safety, these materials should be light, unbreakable, and have no removable parts, sharp edges, or points. As with all materials for this age, they should be thoroughly washable.

### Audiovisual materials

Older infants continue to respond to many of the songs and rhythms that younger infants enjoy (see p. 23). By 7 to 12 months, they can hear differences in "sentence tunes," may try to imitate sounds and sound sequences, and may make singing sounds to music. In addition, the 9- to 12-month-old likes and remembers games such as So Big, This Little Pig, and Pat-a-cake.

Appropriate audiovisual equipment for this age range includes records, tapes, or compact discs with appropriate gentle rhythms, tunes, and songs. The older infant may now notice music boxes as the source of interesting sounds and may want to handle them. Because infants are too young to operate the mechanisms and music boxes typically are not designed to be safe for handling by young children, such equipment is not appropriate for this age group.

## *Gross motor play materials*

Some simple play materials can help older infants begin to develop their gross motor skills.

### Push and pull toys

Materials for the child to pull or push begin to be appropriate when the child is able to move around, either crawling or walking, in the period between 7 and 12 months. When infants begin to creep or crawl, they can use toys that are pushed along on the floor. These early push toys should be simple, undetailed objects of a size and shape easy for grasping. They should be on large, easily turned wheels or rollers. Cars and animals are common designs, and infants prefer objects that make interesting noises as they are pushed along or those that have special visual effects or actions (eyes that turn, heads that bob, etc.). For safety, push toys for this age group should not have handles or strings and should have no small, removable parts.

### Balls and sports equipment

Balls are the earliest form of sports equipment that is appropriate for children. Clutch balls may be used by an infant who has learned to grasp, and they continue to be a favorite grasping toy for the sitting infant. Balls

---

### ☑ Safety Check

Safety precautions to take with mobile infants include

- covering all electrical outlets;
- keeping floors clean and free of tripping hazards;
- removing or securing unstable furniture or objects that can be turned over;
- covering/padding sharp edges that are dangerous if fallen on;
- making certain that all reachable objects in the environment are safe for handling, mouthing, falling on, etc. and conform to the U.S. Consumer Product Safety Commission safety standards for this age range (see pp. 12–14).

---

should be lightweight and made of soft materials, such as cloth, foam (covered so that mouthing infants cannot chew off pieces), or plastic. The best size for balls for this age range is about 5 inches in diameter, for easy grasping. The surface of the ball should be irregular, to provide "handles" for grasping. Balls that produce sounds (chime balls or those that squeak when squeezed) or interesting visual effects (transparent balls with moving parts inside, flutter balls, and action balls) when manipulated or rolled are also interesting to older infants.

## Outdoor and gym equipment

Most gym equipment is not appropriate until the child is walking. Two exceptions are swings and crawling platforms (shown below). Infants who can sit unsupported enjoy being gently pushed in a swing by an adult. Swings used for infants should be appropriate for the size of the child and have backs, sides, and secure front fastenings. Infants should be pushed in gentle, low arcs by an

| Overview of Play Materials for Older Infants— | |
|---|---|
| **Social and Fantasy Play Materials** | **Exploration and Mastery Play Materials** |
| **Mirrors**<br>well-secured wall mirrors (rounded edges; unbreakable)<br>hand mirrors (light; sturdy; unbreakable)<br>**Dolls**<br>soft-bodied or rag dolls (lightweight; painted, stitched, or molded hair and features)<br>**Puppets**<br>simple hand puppets (for holding and moving by adults; safe and washable if grasped by the infant—of visual and social interest)<br>**Stuffed toys/play animals**<br>washable soft animals (simple in design; bright colors; contrasting features that are painted, stitched, or molded)<br>soft rubber or vinyl animals (6–8 inches)—few for grasping and exploring<br>**Transportation toys**<br>(for sitting and mobile infants)<br>simple, one-piece vehicles/cars (6–8 inches; with large wheels or rollers; lightweight rounded/molded appearance; may make noise when pushed) | **Grasping toys**<br>(small hand-held manipulables)<br>teethers<br>beads on rings<br>rubber/plastic pop beads<br>squeeze-squeak toys<br>light, sturdy cloth toys<br>disks, keys on ring<br>interlocking rings (few)<br>grasping/nipple balls<br>toys on suction cups (when sitting)<br>roly-poly toys<br>drop objects on strings<br>**Sand/water play materials**<br>simple floating objects (for bath play)<br>**Construction materials**<br>a few lightweight blocks (soft cloth, rubber, rounded plastic or wood cubes for grasping and stacking; 2–5 inches on a side)<br>**Puzzles**<br>simple, 2–3-piece fit-together objects used as grasping toys<br>**Specific skill-development materials**<br>pop-up boxes (easy operation)<br>simple activity boxes/cubes<br>texture pads<br>simple nesting cups (3–5 cups)<br>stacking ring cones (3–5 rings)<br>containers (with objects) to empty and fill<br>**Books**<br>cloth, plastic, small cardboard picture books (6–8 inches)<br>simple picture books and rhyme books for lap reading |

adult and should never be left unattended. Infants need careful monitoring—for safety and because they vary in their enjoyment of this activity; some may become frightened at any but the slowest, gentlest movements.

Crawling platforms (shown on p. 39) are appropriate for children who can crawl and climb. They should be made of soft material, such as soft foam that is covered with cloth or vinyl. Platforms should be low (no more than 4 to 6 inches high) and wide (enough to accommodate the infant's whole body in any direction) for safe crawling.

## 7 through 12 Months

| Music, Art, and Movement Play Materials | Gross Motor Play Materials |
|---|---|
| **Art and craft materials**<br>(from about 9 to 12 months)<br>a few large, nontoxic crayons<br>large paper taped to a surface<br>**Musical instruments**<br>bell on handle<br>wrist/ankle bells<br>rattles or materials that make a sound when shaken<br>simple, lightweight banging materials<br>**Audiovisual materials**<br>adult-operated players and records, tapes, CDs, etc. with simple repeating rhythms, rhymes, and songs | **Push and pull toys**<br>push toys without rods (simple cars, animals on large wheels or rollers<br>**Balls and sports equipment**<br>balls—clutch and texture balls, chime balls, flutter balls, action balls<br>**Outdoor and gym equipment**<br>swings sized to fit infant, with backs, sides, and front closings—supervised and gently pushed by adults (for infants sitting securely)<br>low soft or padded climbing platforms for crawling infants |

Although the four categories provide a useful classification, play materials can typically be used in more than one way and could be listed under more than one of the categories.

## Priorities and special considerations _____

**Priorities** for play materials for infants 7 through 12 months include providing

- a range of interesting things to explore and manipulate;
- materials that allow the infant to produce interesting effects;
- materials that reward early attempts at mastery;

```
┌─────────────────────────────────────────┐
│              Taking Stock               │
├─────────────────────────────────────────┤
│        Infants 7 through 12 months      │
├─────────────────────────────────────────┤
│                                         │
│    Basic play materials for older infants: │
│                                         │
│  ❏ large, unbreakable mirror(s) placed so that │
│    children can see themselves move     │
│                                         │
│  ❏ a few soft, washable dolls and stuffed or other │
│    play animals                         │
│                                         │
│  ❏ a small selection of soft, lightweight blocks │
│                                         │
│  ❏ a variety of grasping toys that require different │
│    types of manipulation                │
│                                         │
│  ❏ a varied selection of skill-development materi- │
│    als, including nesting and stacking materials, │
│    activity boxes, and containers to be filled and │
│    emptied                              │
│                                         │
│  ❏ a variety of small cloth, plastic, or cardboard │
│    books for children to handle, and additional │
│    books for adults to read             │
│                                         │
│  ❏ a few varied bells and rattles that produce │
│    interesting sounds when manipulated  │
│                                         │
│  ❏ some recorded music, songs, and interesting │
│    sounds                               │
│                                         │
│  ❏ several types of one-piece push toys (cars, │
│    animals) for children who can crawl  │
│                                         │
│  ❏ a variety of balls, including some with interest- │
│    ing special effects                  │
│                                         │
│  ❏ a climbing platform for crawlers     │
│                                         │
└─────────────────────────────────────────┘
```

- materials that support the development of perceptual, fine motor, and gross motor skills;

- materials that support the infant's developing self-awareness, social awareness, and social responsiveness; and

- materials and a play environment that are safe.

Children enjoy variety but can be overwhelmed by too many materials, especially if a large proportion of them are unfamiliar. There should be enough play materials for the size of the group, however, so that each child has a variety of choices available.

Play possibilities, as well as hazards, increase during this period, as eager but inexperienced explorers experiment with their budding skills and reach out to a wider environment. The environment must be carefully checked as children begin to move around in it.

Safety remains a primary consideration when choosing play materials for this age group. Children develop at different rates, and safety frequently is related to what the child can do. There are broad standards for all children younger than age 3 (see pp. 12–14 and 39), but staff must constantly monitor children's motor and cognitive development, the way children are using toys in the environment, and the condition of each toy in terms of cleanliness and state of repair (wood toys can splinter, plastic toys can crack, etc.). Because infants frequently mouth objects during this period, all play materials should be *frequently* cleaned—before being used by another child, whenever possible.

**Special considerations** in group care for older as well as younger infants include *cost, children's health,* and *safety.* Cost should be weighed against the safety and durability of materials for this (and all) age groups. Play materials used by many children need to be especially sturdy. It is important that the materials do not break, crack, chip, or splinter, and that they have a rounded, molded construction for infant and toddler play. Materials do not have to be expensive, but they should be durable, and very inexpensive items may not meet all safety standards. Household items such as sturdy nesting bowls and cups make appropriate play materials when they meet all the criteria for safety. Homemade materials can also be used, but they must meet these demanding standards.

Health remains a major consideration throughout the infant and young toddler years, when resistance to disease is low and children regularly put things in their mouths. Selecting *easily* cleanable materials is especially important when infants are mobile and materials are used by several children in sequence. An important selection criterion for all materials used by children in this age range is the ability to withstand very frequent washing and disinfecting.

# Young Toddlers
# (1 year old)

**YOUNG TODDLERS**

## Abilities and play interests _____

An overview of typical abilities and play interests of young toddlers in the second year of life, that is, 12–24 months—in the motor, perceptual-cognitive, and social-linguistic domains—is outlined below to provide a background for considering appropriate play materials. Keeping in mind the developmental variability among children as a function of both biological and experiential differences, teachers and other staff members selecting play materials for young toddlers need to consider the characteristics of the children they serve. The specific skills and interests of the group affect not only the selection of materials but the plans teachers make for their use.

### *Motor*

- exercises physical skills
- likes to lug, dump, push, pull, pile, knock down, empty, fill
- enjoys pushing or pulling while walking
- likes to climb and can manage small indoor stairs
- manipulates in a more exploratory than skillful fashion
- shows interest in multiple small objects
- carries play materials from place to place
- (by 2 years) kicks and catches a large ball
- (by 2 years) strings large beads, turns knobs, uses twist motion

### *Perceptual-cognitive*

- shows interest in causing effects
- shows curiosity by constantly experimenting with objects
- shows interest in mechanisms and objects that move or can be moved—prefers action toys
- combines objects with other objects—makes simple block structures, uses simple stacking toys, does simple puzzles, puts pegs in pegboard
- shows understanding of simple functional relationships—spoon in bowl or mouth, blanket on doll
- shows interest in hidden-object toys

- (by 18 months to 2 years) groups/matches similar objects—enjoys simple sorting toys
- enjoys sand and water play
- makes marks on paper, scribbles spontaneously

## *Social-linguistic*

- plays in a mostly solitary (rather than social) way; relates to adults better than to children (although experience playing with other children is a factor)
- shows increasing independence
- engages in first imitative play, including imitation of adult tasks, especially caretaking and housekeeping tasks
- expresses affection for others; shows preference for certain soft toys, dolls
- likes being read to and looking at picture books; likes nursery rhymes
- identifies objects by pointing—identifies pictures in a book
- (by 18 months) enjoys interactive games, such as tag

# Initial appropriateness considerations _____

Toddlers are increasingly mobile and interested in practicing their motor skills. Large motor materials (ride-on equipment, push and pull toys, low climbing structures) and those that can be used in combination with large motor activities (balls; large, lightweight blocks) support developing skills, and children enjoy them.

Young toddlers also like to carry play materials around with them or move them from place to place. As toddlers' motor skill improves, their interest in mastery increases, and they are particularly attracted to materials that produce interesting visual effects, movements, or sounds when manipulated. Toddlers are very curious and constantly experiment with objects. They can operate more complex mechanisms than infants and want more challenge and variety in their play materials.

As their ability to imitate and pretend increases, toddlers are beginning to be interested in play objects that resemble "real" things in the world around them. They try to perform the routine cleaning, eating, and caregiving routines they observe, and play materials can support these efforts. Toddlers need time and space for solitary exploration, but they also need frequent interaction with adults. Adults can extend exploratory, mastery, and pretend play repertoires, as well as support language development and social interaction skills.

Children develop an increasing interest in peer interaction during this period, but their skills are limited, and these interactions need careful facilitation and monitoring. Disputes over materials are increasingly common, so providing a number and variety of materials appropriate for

the size of the group is important. Equipment that several children can enjoy together and generic materials that can be used in different ways or in different combinations may also help to minimize friction between children.

# Suggestions for appropriate materials

Now children are up and walking, and they have acquired many new motor, cognitive, and linguistic abilities and interests. With the broadened horizons opened up by their mobility and independence, toddlers are ready for many new play materials.

## Social and fantasy play materials

During the second year, social and fantasy play materials can support the development of simple pretend activities and interactions with peers.

### Mirrors

Full-length (unbreakable and securely mounted) mirrors are suitable for toddlers because they have begun to stand and move about and are increasingly aware of themselves. By approximately 20 months, children begin to enjoy dressing up and seeing themselves in various hats, scarves, etc. Very sturdy, unbreakable, hand-held mirrors with no sharp edges or parts (like mirrors that are appropriate for older infants) are also appropriate for this age range.

### Dolls

Some of the soft, simple dolls appropriate for infants can also be used for young toddlers. At this age, however, children begin to want a more realistic baby doll for their first pretend play, and vinyl or rubber baby dolls become appropriate. These dolls still should be of simple construction. Dolls with hair or moving eyes are not recommended because they are less sturdy, more difficult to clean, and too complex for this age group, and some young toddlers are frightened by moving eyes. Clothes should be simple and need not be detachable, because most children at this age are not capable of dressing a doll (although they may be able to remove simple clothes). Baby dolls should be small enough to hold and carry around in one hand. Children between 18 and 24 months may also begin to play with peg dolls (see "Play Scenes," p. 51). Simple accessories such as blankets, baby bottles or cups, and washcloths are also useful to support pretend caregiving.

Dolls should reflect human diversity, with a variety of skin, hair, and eye colors. Because doll play is largely imitative in this age range, the dolls, doll clothes, and accessories provided for play should reflect the variety that is familiar to the children in the program. As children grow older and their experience broadens, greater variety can be introduced.

### Role-play materials

True fantasy and pretend play begins between 1 and 2 years of age. Children talk into toy telephones, pretend to feed dolls and stuffed animals, enjoy dressing up, wrap up dolls and put them to bed, and pretend to sleep, eat, or wash themselves. By 24 months, they have a definite interest in the mother–child relationship and in domestic mimicry. They can transform objects into toy subjects (a doll is a baby, a piece of wood is a boat) and can make toys carry out actions (eating, drinking). In this age range, children need objects to support their role playing. Objects with some functional and representational details help children with relatively undeveloped representational capacities carry out thematic pretend sequences. Young toddlers are drawn to play objects that have important features of the real object— for example, to serve as a grocery cart, an object needs wheels and some concavity that can hold items. Such objects support children's developing imitative play.

Appropriate role-play materials for this age group (in addition to mirrors, dolls, stuffed toys, and the like, discussed in previous sections) include doll bottles and feeding items, a doll cradle or bed (big and sturdy enough for a child to get into), doll blankets, a baby carriage (big and sturdy enough for a child to ride in—see "Ride-on equipment" pp. 58–59), a play telephone, a set of sturdy housecleaning items that work, play dishes, sturdy pots and pans with covers, child-sized tables and chairs, a child-sized rocking chair, a child-sized playhouse, and simple dress-up materials (purses, ties, scarves). A play stove, sink, cupboard, ironing board and iron, and cutlery may be added at around 24 months. For safety, all materials for this age group should be very sturdy, thoroughly cleanable, and have no sharp edges or points or swallowable parts.

### Puppets

Toddlers do not engage in true puppet play in the sense of imaginative or fantasy play with puppets. They enjoy soft, plush, stuffed puppets that double as stuffed animals, but there may be competition for these items in a group setting, and they are difficult to keep clean. Simple, washable hand puppets may be used in interaction with adults who support the play. These should be small—8 to 12 inches—and lightweight. The hand opening should be sized for the toddler's small hand span. Hand-and-arm puppets are generally too long for this age group, and toddlers do not have sufficient dexterity to operate puppets with arms.

Puppets for this age range need not be highly detailed or realistic, but young toddlers prefer puppets that represent familiar human or animal forms. Contrasting facial features are important, especially eyes.

### Stuffed toys/play animals

Stuffed and soft floppy "cuddly" toys often become more interesting and attractive to children between 1 and 2 years of age. Young toddlers may select and carry around a favorite object of this type. This may prove problematic in a group setting, and keeping such materials clean can be difficult, but problems must be weighed against the comfort that the objects give to children. Children may also use stuffed toys in their pretend play.

Rubber or vinyl play animals can be interesting to toddlers and may be used in play scenes. Children carry them around like other easily portable play materials.

**YOUNG TODDLERS**

### Play scenes

Children younger than 18 months may enjoy handling or carrying around little toy people and animals or doing simple relational activities, such as placing small peg people into small cars, boats, or other simple representational materials. After about 18 months, children may pretend with objects that include constructing and/or playing with miniature play scenes.

During the 18-to-24 month period, toddlers begin to develop the mental representation necessary for more complex fantasy play with objects and the small muscle coordination necessary for setting up scenes, moving figures in and out of structures, and the like. They may begin to make objects act upon other objects. Play scenes begin to be appropriate at this time. (Larger materials for supporting this kind of play are described under "Role-play materials," p. 50). The materials for representing scenes must be familiar and realistic enough for recognition and simple functional use by the child. The materials need not have minute detail or many figures and accessories; too many materials may be confusing or overwhelming to toddlers. Play-scene materials for this age need only have four to six figures (materials that can be used for people, animals, vehicles, etc.) and additional materials that can be used to represent a simple, familiar situation (e.g., a garage, a barn, an airplane, a bus).

Materials used to support early thematic pretend play should have more identifying representational features than do materials for older children, who can construct a variety of play scenes out of relatively unstructured materials, such as blocks or Legos. For young toddlers, objects should also be lightweight enough for the child to carry or move around easily and made of washable, unbreakable plastic or lightweight wood with rounded edges.

### Transportation toys

Between 8 and 12 months, children begin to understand the social meaning of toys and become interested in transportation toys as familiar objects. Play materials representing cars, trucks, airplanes, boats, etc. should have sufficient detail to be recognizable as what they are meant to be, unlike the generic vehicles on rollers appropriate for infants. Cars and trucks should be 6 to 8 inches or smaller for easy grasping and carrying. Soft plastic and hard rubber are still the preferred materials. Wooden vehicles are appropriate if they are not too heavy. Children at this age usually are capable of manually pushing or pulling vehicles, as well as pushing vehicles with rods. After about 18 months, when they are steady walkers, children can pull cars or trains on short strings, no longer than 12 inches.

Twelve- to 18-month-old toddlers also enjoy simple trains. First trains should be very simple—1 to 3 cars made out of molded plastic or wood and not highly detailed (although they should be recognizable as trains). Trains for children of this age should be powered by the child's push. Most children are not capable of working even the simplest coupling mechanism. The trains need not even have wheels, and tracks are not appropriate. From about 18 months, children may successfully use multi-car trains and be able to use simple coupling mechanisms (nonsharp hooks or magnet fastenings). They may also be interested in simple detachable or removable parts.

Toddlers' interest in functioning parts and representative detail increases in the 18-to-24-month period. Among the kinds of details that are appropriate are doors that open and shut and vehicle parts that move up and down. These parts should be designed so as to not pinch or trap fingers and to be very sturdy. Simple accessories—objects that can be put into and carried by trucks—are also interesting to toddlers and support their pretend play.

## Exploration and mastery play materials

As young toddlers become increasingly capable of exploring the environment, materials for exploration and experimentation can support and nourish their developing interest and skills.

### Grasping toys

During the second year, children lose interest in all but the most complex grasping toys. They now become interested in more complex manipulations involving dials, switches, knobs, and the like, and in more complex manipulables (see "Specific skill-development materials," p. 55). They are interested in putting things together and taking them apart, in fitting things into other things, and in hidden objects and surprise, or "pop-up," materials (shown on p. 56).

### Sand and water play materials

For toddlers from 12 to 18 months, recommendations for sand and water play materials are similar to those for older infants. Simple, small (4- to 6-inch) floating objects are appropriate. Toddlers are more interested in what

the object represents than are younger children, and they prefer familiar, recognizable objects.

In the latter half of the second year, a wider variety of water play materials become appropriate, including multipart materials for exploration and experimentation with water and materials that can be used for fantasy play. These items appeal to children's increasing interest in creating effects, combining objects, and engaging in pretend play with objects. Water activity centers are interesting to toddlers in this age range, but they should involve only simple-action mechanisms (hinged doors, buttons to push, simple levers), and parts should be at least 2 to 4 inches in size for the child to manipulate them successfully. The activity centers should be attached firmly to the side of a tub or pool by an adult. Young toddlers enjoy using nesting cups, funnels, colanders, and sprinkling cans in their water play. Simple fantasy play materials (floating fish to catch in cups or colanders, peg people to put in and out of boats, etc.) are also very interesting to toddlers. Water materials should be made of lightweight, unbreakable materials, such as plastic or rubber. Toddlers may chew pieces off sponges, and most wood materials are too heavy for easy manipulation in water. Although group water tubs and tables have been traditionally used with young children, the medical community is now recommending the use of individual tubs to reduce the possibility of children catching infection from others.

Sand play materials become appropriate during the second year. Sand tools for this age include shovels, rakes with blunt teeth, buckets, and other small containers. When children sit in sand or stand at a sand table, they need smaller-sized tools. Older toddlers who are steady on their feet can use large tools in an outdoor sand area.

## Construction materials

At around 1 year, children may begin to make combinations for a few (two or three) objects. The simple, lightweight blocks recommended for infants are appropriate for the young toddler, especially in the 12-to-18-month age range. Blocks for children older than 12 months may be somewhat smaller (2 to 4 inches) than those for infants. Children who are producing only simple combinations, such as small stacks or rows, need only a few rather than a large array of blocks.

Most 12-to-18-month-olds are unable to master the action used to connect parts of interlocking building materials, so only the simplest connecting systems are appropriate for children 18 to 24 months of age. Among the earliest interlocking systems that can be used successfully by toddlers are pieces that can be easily and randomly pressed together, such as bristle blocks. Because children do not build elaborate structures at this age, they still do not need a large number of blocks of any type. Starter sets of 20 to 30 pieces are usually sufficient, depending on how many children will be using the materials at the same time.

Opinions differ on the age at which solid wooden unit blocks are appropriate, because of the potential dangers associated with toddlers handling heavy blocks without rounded edges. Although some people believe that children as young as 18 months to 2 years of age are able to use these blocks safely and productively, most early childhood specialists consider them suitable only for children of 2 and older.

## Puzzles

By the age of 12 months, children may be interested in simple pre-puzzles. These items should have only two or three pieces and should fit together easily. Thick plastic pieces with rounded edges are most useful because they are mouthable and washable. Young toddlers also enjoy wood or plastic puzzle blocks. Contrasting colors on different pieces help the child perceive their relationship and "fit." After 18 months, with an increasing interest in mastery, children may put things together and work to complete shape-sorting boxes, form boards, and simple puzzles with three to five pieces. Puzzles should be of the fit-in variety, with pieces fitting easily into pre-cut outline forms. Knobs on the pieces are also useful, but they should be very sturdy and firmly attached.

## Dressing, lacing, and stringing materials

Young toddlers may be able to learn to string large wood or plastic beads (shown below), but they are most successful at these activities after 18 months of age. By this time their pincer grasp has developed, and children are interested in the purposeful use of objects. After 18 months, children can lace with lacing cubes or boards that have thick string and a thick, blunt spindle to push through the holes. The holes should be large and easy to push through. For safety, strings should be less than 12 inches long, and the cubes and boards should have rounded edges.

## Pattern-making materials

Toddlers are not cognitively ready to make patterns, but they play with materials that will later be used for this purpose. They may fit a few large (wood or plastic) pegs into forms or boards (wood, plastic, or foam) with holes. This activity prepares them for later pegboard activities.

## Specific skill-development materials

From 12 to 18 months, children are very interested in operating mechanisms, in looking for hidden objects, in fitting things into other things, and in putting pieces together and taking them apart. Young toddlers can open lids or doors and manipulate dials, switches, and knobs. All of these activities help increase sensory perception and discrimination and support developing fine motor skills.

After 18 months, children become increasingly purposeful in their use of objects. They are interested in pop-up boxes (shown on p. 56), shape sorters, form boards, simple puzzles, and more complex nesting materials. They also like simple pounding and hammering materials, although these items must be carefully selected and monitored for safety. In the latter half of the second year, toddlers may nest or stack four or five pieces correctly and may fit three or four shapes into a shape sorter. Slightly more complex stacking and nesting materials (round canisters and cubes) are also appropriate. Toddlers in this age range are particularly interested in finding objects in closed or closable containers, so play materials that feature objects inside other objects may now completely cover the contained objects. During the 18-to-24-month period, children can use the pincer grasp and are learning the screwing/unscrewing action. They may open containers that require a rotation motion, although most toddlers can make only one turn in opening a container. From 18 to 24 months, toddlers may successfully use simple cylinder blocks and number pegboards with one to five large pegs. They may operate very simple lock boxes and lock-and-key toys. Very simple matching and lotto activities with just a few pieces may also be introduced.

## Books

Books appropriate for young toddlers include cloth, plastic, and cardboard books for the children to look at independently (or with an adult) and other, more fragile books for lap reading with an adult. Most suitable are picture books, simple picture/storybooks (with few words or one line per page), and nursery rhyme books.

By about 19 months, children are ready for "touch me" and other tactile books and books with heavy paper pages. They may now name and point to familiar objects in books, and they particularly like listening to simple rhymes and trying to repeat them with adults.

## *Music, art, and movement materials*

During the second year, toddlers show an increasingly active interest in and response to simple art, music, and movement activities.

### Art and craft materials

By the age of 16 months, toddlers may scribble in imitation, and many will scribble spontaneously. By around 18 months, toddlers usually display a hand preference, and most toddlers scribble spontaneously. They make circular, horizontal, and vertical marks and may make a crude *V* by about 24 months. Scribbling is enjoyed at this point and may support developing representational abilities. Large, nontoxic preschool crayons and large, sturdy papers are appropriate for these early drawing activities.

### Musical instruments

From about 15 months, children may enjoy true rhythm instruments, such as bells and rattles. Although some toddlers will bang on a drum with two sticks at around 18 to 24 months, they tend to use the drum as a hammering toy rather than as a musical instrument. Instruments for this age should be very sturdy and have a rounded, molded appearance, with no sharp edges or small parts.

### Audiovisual materials

Thirteen-month-old children sometimes sing to themselves and may listen to rhymes and jingles for three minutes or more. At around 14 months, toddlers bounce to music. Children who are nearly 2 years old enjoy hearing live or recorded music (repeating and rhythmic instrumental tunes, simple songs, and simple nursery or other rhymes). They are generally interested in sounds and repetition. Their "dancing" to music may include bouncing, running, turning in circles, and bounding. By 18 to 24 months, toddlers may enjoy simple point-to and finger-play games and songs. Live instruments or recordings (tapes, records, CDs) support these activities.

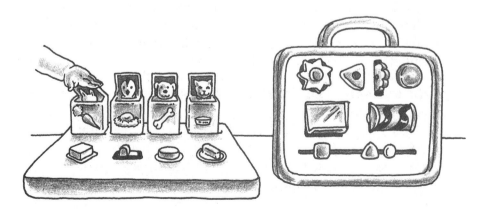

## Gross motor play materials

Increasing mobility and developing gross motor skills make appropriate gross motor play materials interesting to young toddlers and useful for practicing their skills.

### Push and pull toys

In the period when children are improving their walking skills, push toys that have rigid rods with handles attached become appropriate. These can function as aids to walking, because a wobbly toddler can use the stick as a balancing stabilizer. For the same reason, small four-wheeled vehicles with high upright handles for pushing also can be used by unsteady walkers. To use pull toys with cords (no more than 12 inches long, for safety), children need to be steady walkers, and this usually occurs only after 18 months. Pull toys on cords do not provide any support, and to be fully experienced, they require the child to look back while walking. Also, the cord can get caught on objects or wrapped around the toddler's legs, so pull toys require more advanced control than push toys.

Appropriate push and pull toys for young toddlers share many of the same characteristics as those for infants. They should be simple in design and operation. Children often favor recognizable objects, such as dogs, but enjoy any toy that makes interesting noises or visual effects as it moves along. Children of this age delight in producing effects, and "action" push and pull toys gratify this interest.

Push and pull toys should be sturdy—either wooden or heavy plastic. Push toys must have rigid rods with large, blunt handles that the child can grasp easily and not be injured by if she falls. Pull toys should have sufficient weight to slightly resist the child's pull and should be broad based, with a low center of gravity to avoid tipping.

In the latter half of the child's second year, two additional kinds of push and pull toys become appropriate: simple carriages and wagons. These items are appropriate not only because the child is now sufficiently coordinated to handle them but also because the child's interest in pretend play is increasing, and these toys are excellent props for a variety of play scenarios. First wagons and carriages should be relatively small and open so that the child has easy access to loading and unloading. They do not need to be highly detailed. Simple, sturdy vehicles are most appropriate. For safety, all edges should be rounded.

### Balls and sports equipment

During the first half of the second year, some children are beginning to be able to play simple ball games, either grasping and letting go of a ball or to-and-from activities. By around 18 months, children may begin to hurl a ball. Young toddlers enjoy the same kinds of soft, small, lightweight balls that are appropriate for infants. In addition, they like large, lightweight balls, such as beach balls. Children at this age are interested in the movements of varying types and sizes of balls and are fascinated by balls that roll in unpredictable ways, such as a football or a ball weighted to roll oddly. Balls should be no smaller than 1¼ inches in diameter to avoid being a choking hazard. During the latter part of this period, children's new skills with balls commonly include kicking and throwing, and they may be interested in tossing or throwing a ball at a target.

## Ride-on equipment

After learning to walk proficiently, toddlers become capable of using ride-on toys, such as kiddie cars, that they straddle and can propel by pushing. Young toddlers may not be capable of alternating their feet in pushing and may propel the ride-on vehicle by pushing both feet simultaneously. The ability to pedal rarely emerges before age 2½ to 3 years.

For safety, ride-on toys must be stable, and vehicles with four or more wheels tend to be more stable than three- or two-wheeled vehicles. Wheels should be spaced relatively wide apart (wide enough to be stable) but not so wide as to make it difficult for the child to swing a leg over the seat. The ride-on toy should be low (at about the child's knee height) for easy mounting, and the child's feet should be flat on the floor when he is seated. Recessed casters or wheels make the ride-on toy easier for the child to maneuver without banging feet or legs into them. For very young children, casters may be preferable, because they will permit movement in any direction without tipping. The first ride-ons do not have to have steering mechanisms, because very young toddlers may be unable to use them effectively. The child at 18 to 24 months may be able to operate ride-ons that he sits inside, such as cars, and propels the toy by pushing with his feet. These vehicles are more difficult to use than the straddle ride-ons, however, because they are harder to get into and maneuver.

Some features of ride-on toys increase their interest or play value for toddlers. Bright colors and special sound effects (noises produced as a vehicle moves, or ones that the child can effect, such as with horns) make ride-ons more attractive to this age range. Ride-ons with walker handles on the back may function as walking aids for young toddlers. Ride-ons with storage bins or trays add play value, because toddlers are interested in collecting and carrying around multiple items. Although representational characteristics are not necessary, ride-ons made to look like animals or vehicles are especially popular.

Rocking and bouncing (typically "horse") ride-ons can be introduced to children in the latter half of the second year. They should be small enough for the child to mount and dismount easily and low enough that the child is unlikely to be hurt by falling off. The child's feet should touch the floor when she is seated on the ride-on. This type of ride-on equipment should have a confined rocking arc and a gentle bounce for toddlers.

For the most part, "walkers," which differ from ride-on toys, are considered unsafe by a great many pediatricians.

### Outdoor and gym equipment

During the second year, most children learn to walk and climb with increasing proficiency. In the second half of this period, toddlers become very interested in exploring and exploiting their capacities for gross motor movement. They are especially interested in exploring positions in space and particularly like the experience of being up high. They may be able to climb a 3-step ladder or go up a few stairs, although they may have difficulty coming down. Some toddlers can also descend a small, low slide. Considering the motor development of the children in a program is especially important when deciding what gym equipment to make available for their use.

Appropriate equipment for this age range typically includes simple, low climbing platforms (made of carpeted wood or covered foam) and safely designed and secured "tunnels" to crawl through. Low toddler stairs with handrails and low slides with siderails may be appropriate from 18 months. Toddlers also enjoy the sensation of swinging. Swings for toddlers should be low, and swing seats should be curved or "body shaped" rather than flat boards. They should be made of an energy-absorbing material, such as rubber or canvas.

Toddlers typically have poor judgment about the consequences of actions and may easily hurt themselves or others. For safety, *the use of all gross motor equipment must be constantly supervised by an adult.*


## Priorities and special considerations _____

**Priorities** for play materials for young toddlers 1 year of age include providing an appropriate range of materials to support and nurture children's

- rapidly expanding fine and gross motor capacities;
- increased interest in active exploration and mastery of objects and their own capacities;
- interest in ordering and predicting events in their environments (for instance, growing interest in repeated routines);
- desire for independence;
- growing awareness of, imitation of, and responsiveness to others; and
- beginning capacity for engaging in pretend and role-play activities.

| Social and Fantasy Play Materials | Exploration and Mastery Play Materials |
|---|---|
| **Mirrors**<br>well-secured wall mirrors (rounded edges, unbreakable)<br>full-length (upright), unbreakable mirror, firmly mounted or in nontippable stand<br>hand mirrors (light, sturdy, unbreakable)<br><br>**Dolls**<br>soft-bodied or washable rubber/vinyl baby dolls<br>simple accessories for caregiving: bottle, blanket<br>simple doll clothes—need not be detachable (lightweight; painted, stitched, or molded hair and features; no moving eyes or articulated limbs; sized to fit easily in child's arms: 6 or 8–13 inches)<br><br>(from about 18 months)<br>small peg people (not swallowable)<br><br>**Role-play materials**<br>play telephone<br>simple housekeeping and work-role equipment<br>simple doll equipment—bed, baby carriage (sturdy and large enough to hold child)<br><br>**Puppets**<br>puppets operated by adult<br><br>(from about 18 months)<br>small hand puppets, sized to fit child's hand<br><br>**Stuffed toys/play animals**<br>washable, soft animals (simple in design, with bright colors, contrasting features that are painted, stitched, or molded)<br>soft rubber or vinyl animals (6–8 inches)—a few for exploring and beginning pretend play<br><br>**Play scenes**<br>(from about 18 months)<br>small people/animal figures, with simple supporting materials (vehicle, barn) to make familiar scenes<br><br>**Transportation toys**<br>simple, lightweight vehicles (6–8 inches, with large wheels or rollers; lightweight; rounded/molded appearance; may make noise when pushed)<br>first train—1–2 cars, no tracks, simple or no coupling system<br><br>(from about 18 months)<br>more detailed vehicles—can have a few simple, sturdy moving parts (doors or hoods that open)<br>trains with simple coupling system (wood link, large blunt hook, magnet) | **Grasping toys**<br>(toddlers are losing interest in the small, hand-held manipulables enjoyed by infants)<br><br>**Sand/water play materials**<br>simple floating objects, easily grasped in one hand<br>small shovel and pail<br><br>(from about 18 months)<br>nesting materials useful for pouring<br>funnels, colanders<br>water activity centers<br>small sand tools (container with shovel or scoop; rake with blunt teeth)<br><br>**Construction materials**<br>light blocks (soft cloth, rubber, rounded plastic, or wood cubes for grasping and stacking, 2–4 inches on a side)—15–25 pieces<br><br>(from about 18 months)<br>unit blocks (suggested by some experts and teachers)—20–40 pieces<br>large plastic bricks (2–4 inches, press-together type)<br><br>**Puzzles**<br>simple prepuzzles or form boards, 2–3 pieces, in familiar shapes<br><br>(from about 18 months)<br>3–5-piece fit-in puzzles (knobs make them easier to use but must be very firmly attached)<br><br>**Dressing, lacing, stringing materials**<br>large, colored beads (fewer than 10)<br><br>(from about 18 months)<br>lacing cubes or board with thick, blunt spindle<br><br>**Specific skill-development materials**<br>pop-up boxes (easy operation)<br>simple activity boxes/cubes (with doors, lids, switches)<br>nesting cups (with round shapes, few pieces)<br>simple stacking materials—no order necessary<br><br>(from about 18 months)<br>activity boxes with more complex mechanisms (turning knob or dial or simple key)<br>simple lock boxes<br>nesting materials of more complex shapes (square)<br>objects in closed containers that may be opened (by simple screwing action)<br>4–5-piece stacking materials<br>cylinder blocks<br>pegboards (with a few large pegs)<br>simple matching and lotto materials<br><br>**Books**<br>cloth, plastic, or cardboard picture books<br>simple picture and rhyme books with repetition for lap reading<br><br>(from about 18 months)<br>touch-me or tactile books |

# 1 Year Old

**YOUNG TODDLERS**

| Music, Art, and Movement Play Materials | Gross Motor Play Materials |
| --- | --- |
| **Art and craft materials**<br>few large, nontoxic crayons<br>large paper taped to surface<br>**Musical instruments**<br>rhythm instruments for shaking—bells, rattles<br><br>(from about 18 months)<br>rhythm instruments for banging—cymbals, drums<br>**Audiovisual materials**<br>adult-operated players and records, tapes, CDs, etc.<br>  with simple repeating rhythms, rhymes, and songs<br><br>(from about 14 months)<br>music to "dance" (bounce) to<br><br>(from about 18 months)<br>simple "point to" and finger-play games and songs | **Push and pull toys**<br>push toys with rods (rods with large handles<br>  on ends)<br>toys to push along the floor—simple cars,<br>  animals on large wheels or rollers<br>for steady walkers, pull toys on short strings<br>  (broad based to tip less easily)<br><br>(from about 18 months)<br>simple doll carriages and wagons (low, open,<br>  big enough for child to get into)<br>push/pull toys filled with multiple objects<br>**Balls and sports equipment**<br>soft, lightweight balls, especially those with<br>  interesting audio or visual effects (noises,<br>  unpredictable movement)<br>larger balls, including beach ball size<br><br>(from about 18 months)<br>balls for beginning throwing and kicking<br>**Ride-on equipment**<br>stable ride-ons propelled by pushing with feet<br>  (no pedals; no steering mechanism; four or<br>  more wheels spaced wide apart for stability;<br>  child's feet flat on floor when seated)<br>ride-ons with storage bins<br><br>(from about 18 months)<br>bouncing or rocking ride-ons (with confined<br>  rocking arc and gentle bounce for toddlers;<br>  child's feet touch floor when seated)<br>**Outdoor and gym equipment**<br>low, soft or padded climbing platforms<br>tunnels for crawling through<br>swings (pushed and monitored by adult), with<br>  seats curved or body shaped, front closing,<br>  and made of energy-absorbing materials<br><br>(from about 18 months)<br>low toddler stairs with handrails |

Although the four categories provide a useful classification, play materials can typically be used in more than one way and could be listed under more than one of the categories.

☑ **Safety Check**

As children are able to explore with increasing thoroughness, play materials must be safe for their uses and abuses (children may bang, bite, chew, fall on, trip over, etc.). Materials must be very sturdy, meet all safety standards for the age group, and be safe for the children being served. They must also be carefully maintained (examined for breaks, cracks, splinters, etc.) and regularly and thoroughly cleaned.

The environment must be carefully prepared, with

- all electrical outlets covered,

- electric cords removed or moved out of reach,

- floor coverings cleaned and firmly fixed,

- tripping/falling hazards minimized,

- fragile items and furniture with sharp points or edges padded or removed, and

- stairs and hazardous areas or equipment screened off and carefully monitored and maintained.

Safety continues to be an extremely important priority when considering any play materials for children in this age range, who have broadening interests but still limited skills.

Compared with infants, young toddlers not only are more mobile but also are more likely to notice what other children are playing with—and to want what they see. Toddlers also are unlikely to relinquish without strong protest an object that another child tries to take. Moreover, children in this age range have not yet developed the ability to wait, use a toy cooperatively, or take turns. For these reasons, conflicts over toys are common. Although children learn from having some of these conflicts, adults caring for toddlers in groups can reduce friction to a manageable level by carefully planning and selecting materials. Providing a variety of appropriate play materials, with multiples of each type, can reduce sources of friction. Having just one copy of a highly attractive toy is asking for trouble. Caregivers should decide how many of an item to provide on the basis of the number of children in the group and their range of interests and abilities.

Children's increased interest in independence and experimentation requires adults' constant vigilance and careful monitoring of toddlers' activities with even "safe" materials. All materials for this age range must be designed with health and safety in mind, as well as the interests and abilities of children. Play materials must be easily cleanable, be very sturdy (unbreakable), and have no small (swallowable) parts or sharp edges that unstable toddlers could fall on.

**YOUNG TODDLERS**

## Taking Stock

### Toddlers 1 year old

Basic play materials for young toddlers:

❏ a sturdy, unbreakable full-length mirror

❏ a few simple, washable dolls

❏ a few small wood or sturdy plastic people and animal figures

❏ simple dress-ups (kept very clean), and a doll bed and carriage that a toddler can fit into

❏ several lightweight transportation toys (cars, trucks)

❏ simple sand and water play materials (from about 18 months)

❏ a beginning set of small, lightweight blocks and simple, press-together bricks

❏ a variety of 3- to 5-piece puzzles with knobs

❏ a number of large, colored pop beads or stringing beads (after about 18 months)

❏ a variety of specific skill-development materials, including shape-sorters, stacking and nesting materials, pop-up and activity boxes, and simple matching materials

❏ foam/wood/plastic pegboard(s) with large, blunt-ended pegs

❏ a variety of sturdy books for children to handle and additional books for adults to read

❏ a supply of sturdy paper and large, nontoxic crayons in bright, primary colors

❏ a beginning set of simple musical instruments (from about 15 months)

❏ recorded music and a record, CD, or tape player

❏ a variety of push and pull toys

❏ several types and sizes of balls

❏ a few stable ride-on toys with four wheels or casters and no steering mechanism or pedals

❏ low, soft, climbing platform(s) and tunnel for crawling through

The safety of these play materials is related both to the broad safety standards for children younger than 3 (see p. 39) and to specific characteristics of this age group. Children are becoming increasingly mobile and are interested in gross motor activity, but their balance may be precarious. They are also interested in exploring everything and have little understanding of what might be dangerous. Materials should be selected and maintained—and the environment should be prepared and maintained—with these characteristics and the special needs and interests of the children served in mind. Caregivers should also carefully observe children as they play with materials and move about in the environment to ensure that plans for safety are adequate and to monitor changes in children's abilities and interests that affect safety.

**Special considerations** in group programs for young toddlers, as well as for infants, include *cost, children's health,* and *safety.* Cost should be weighed against the safety and durability of materials for this (and all) age groups. Play materials used by many children, especially toddlers, need to be very sturdy. It is important that toys do not break, crack, chip, or splinter if chewed, banged, or stepped on. Household items used for play and bought or constructed play materials must meet all the safety standards for this age range. Household materials (funnels, measuring cups, wooden spoons, strainers, etc., that meet safety standards) can be used for sand and water play, and old clothes (ties, scarves) can be used for dress-up. Books for lap reading can be borrowed from libraries, and used computer paper can serve as paper for drawing. Simple rhythm instruments can also be constructed from household or recycled items. Simple matching games can be made from cut-out pictures pasted on cardboard and covered with contact paper. Picture books can also be made this way and put together on rings.

Health remains a major consideration throughout the infant and young toddler years, when children regularly put things in their mouths. Mobile toddlers who use the same materials may mouth toys in sequence. Selecting easily cleanable toys is especially important for this age group, and extra efforts to keep shared materials clean helps prevent the spread of disease.

# Chapter 5

# Older Toddlers
# (2 years old)

## Abilities and play interests _____

To provide a background for considering appropriate play materials for older toddlers, an overview of typical abilities and play interests of children 2 years of age—in the motor, perceptual-cognitive, and social-linguistic domains—is outlined below. As always, it is important to remember that not all children in this age range demonstrate all of the abilities and interests mentioned. Because developmental rates vary, the skills and interests of individual children may resemble those of younger or older children. In addition, the skills and interests of children develop in interaction with their environments, so culture and individual experiences increasingly affect their play. As children get older, they increasingly recognize and come to expect the features and processes (regularities, routines, responses/reactions) they have previously experienced. Small deviations from learned expectancies can be exciting and challenging, but large differences can be confusing or frightening. It is increasingly important, therefore, to take children's previous experiences into account, as well as their current observed abilities and interests, when selecting play materials and planning for their use. As children get older, cultural and experiential appropriateness of materials should match children's interests and support their developing understanding of themselves and the social and physical world around them.

### *Motor*

- shows skill in most simple large muscle activities
- engages in lots of physical testing: jumping from heights, climbing, hanging by the arms, rolling, galloping, doing somersaults, rough-and-tumble play
- throws and retrieves all kinds of objects
- pushes self on wheeled objects with good steering
- demonstrates good hand and finger coordination by 2½ to 3 years
- engages in lots of active play with small objects and explores different qualities of play materials

## Perceptual-cognitive

- shows interest in attributes of objects—texture, shape, size, color
- matches a group of similar objects
- plays with pattern, sequence, order of size; may begin to copy patterns (two to four pieces)
- demonstrates first counting skills
- demonstrates first creative activities (drawing, constructing, molding clay) but is less interested in the final product than in the process
- uses objects to carry out actions on other objects (makes a doll pat a toy animal)
- is beginning to work out problem solutions mentally rather than by using trial-and-error

## Social-linguistic

- engages in imaginative fantasy play more often; shows continued interest in imitating domestic roles
- although primarily interested in adults, begins to play interactively with other children (especially from 30 months) and may engage in some pretend play with others
- sometimes offers play materials to others but is usually protective of materials in own possession and may "hoard" materials (finds choice difficult)
- shows strong desire for independence; displays pride in accomplishment
- uses more language in play and in expressing wishes to others
- enjoys hearing simple stories read from picture books, especially stories with repetition

# Initial appropriateness considerations _____

Older toddlers, 2 years of age, love active, physical play and have significantly more advanced gross motor skills. Their fine motor skills have also improved, and children now manipulate and explore objects with more deliberate experimentation and purposeful efforts at mastery. This increased interest in goal-directed activity may lead them to work for extended periods to operate mechanisms and to create specific effects. Play materials can support this shift in emphasis by incorporating interesting characteristics that can be discovered and by providing appropriate levels of challenge for mastery.

Older toddlers have better developed representational skills. They can use one object to represent another: a block can be a "car" and a stick can be a "broom." They exhibit more complex repertoires of pretend activities, including sequenced episodes such as "feeding" a doll and then putting it to bed. Children older than 2 can also imitate and elaborate on simple patterns they observe in their social and physical environments. They put together materials in more complex and ordered configurations, creating simple patterns and constructions with blocks or other materials. They also are more able to match and sort objects into simple functional and perceptual categories. Play materials can support and nurture growing representational capacities by providing experiences that help the child discover and create patterns. Materials that can be matched, sorted, fitted together, or constructed or arranged in interesting ways are useful. Media that support creative "artistic" representation (paper for making marks on, clay, dough, sand) are also useful and interesting for older toddlers.

**OLDER TODDLERS**

The developing representational abilities of children in this age range are also demonstrated in their pretend play. Providing appropriate materials for pretend and interactive dramatic play is important for older toddlers in order to extend their social understanding and to support their growing interaction skills. A larger variety of fantasy and role-play materials are appropriate in the third than in the second year.

## Suggestions for appropriate materials _____

Not only are older toddlers more advanced in motor abilities, but they also are beginning to engage in pretend play and creative activities of various kinds. An increasing number and variety of play materials have value for their development.

### *Social and fantasy play materials*

Play materials can support the increasingly complex repertoires of pretend play that older toddlers are developing.

### Mirrors

Unbreakable, full-length mounted mirrors or stable mirrors on stands are appropriate for older toddlers. Very sturdy, unbreakable hand mirrors with no sharp edges or parts are also appropriate for this age range.

### Dolls

Most child development experts designate this period as the beginning of true doll play. As the child begins to assign more important meaning and characteristics to the doll, it takes on more complex roles in pretend play. As a result, more representational dolls (that look more like babies or whatever they are intended to be) with more accessories and props become appropriate (particularly as children near 3 years of age). Simple removable clothes with easy-to-fasten (Velcro) closings and simple feeding and care accessories are useful for supporting play. Dolls designed so that they can be washed by children are preferable for pretend play. Most children of this age cannot yet manipulate articulated limbs. Children like rooted hair and moving eyes, but these characteristics make dolls more fragile and harder to clean, which makes them less useful in group settings.

As children begin to notice and appreciate more specific features of dolls, it is especially important that these and all materials for pretend and fantasy play reflect the range of physical and cultural differences observed in the children served and in their familiar environments. Including dolls and accessories that represent unfamiliar characteristics prepares children to appreciate and respect diversity. Especially for young children with limited experience, play materials representing unfamiliar characteristics must be carefully introduced in the environment (via stories and pictures in books, filmstrips and videos, field trips, classroom visits, etc.), in conjunction with experiences that prepare children to meaningfully and positively include these materials in their play.

## Role-play materials

Two-year-old children are developing a self-identity and an awareness of themselves as separate from others, but they are still very egocentric. They are beginning to play with other children but need adult help and supervision during these interactions.

Older toddlers like to pretend to be the mother, the father, the baby, etc. and enjoy playing house. They can change roles during play. By this age, children are better able to imagine objects and can begin to create extra props for pretend play, using blocks or other generic objects (such as a piece of cloth for a blanket or a dress-up cape). Appropriate role-play materials include all of the items appropriate for younger toddlers, with the addition of a washable doll (see "Dolls," starting on p. 69), more doll-play accessories (doll bathtub, simple doll clothes with Velcro or big buttons, doll stroller, and play stove, sink, cupboard, and shopping cart), pots and pans with covers, very sturdy and safe eating utensils, additional cleaning equipment (broom, mop, dustpan, dustcloth, carpet sweeper) that really works, and more dress-ups (vests, dresses, work gloves, suitcase, and very simple doctor, police, or other work-role clothes). Large transportation toys, including those that children can ride on, are also used for role play. For health and safety, all materials should be very sturdy and cleanable, with no sharp edges or points and no swallowable parts.

## Puppets

The puppets appropriate for this age range are nearly identical to those suggested for younger toddlers. Older toddlers are more likely to be interested in puppets that portray familiar persons or characters. They may respond to an adult using a puppet by imitating or interacting with the adult's puppet.

OLDER TODDLERS

### Stuffed toys/play animals

Sturdy wood, rubber, vinyl, or plastic play animals (zoo, farm, and aquatic) are interesting and appropriate for children in this age range. These play materials are useful for language learning and fantasy play and may be incorporated in children's created play scenes with blocks or other materials.

### Play scenes

The play-scene materials suggested for young toddlers are appropriate for 2-year-olds. Small representations of people and animals with a few vehicles and/or enclosures (for rooms, barns, garages, etc.) support children's growing interest in and capacity for fantasy play. Older toddlers can incorporate more different pieces in their play than the four to six pieces used by younger children. Materials should be sturdy and have no sharp edges or small, swallowable parts.

### Transportation toys

Children's interest in vehicles continues to increase during this period. Small cars (3 to 4 inches) are often of particular interest, but they should be very sturdy. Less detailed vehicles are more flexible and can become fire engines, ambulances, delivery trucks, or passenger cars, depending on the child's play needs. Such vehicles also lend themselves to play involving fewer disputes over which child has which toy. Larger vehicles (12 to 15 inches) can also be manipulated successfully and are good for pushing around. Older toddlers also enjoy and can manipulate low, sturdy ride-on vehicles (18 to 24 inches long and 10 to 12 inches high), which can be used with large hollow blocks. Children of this age prefer trucks that have some form of working mechanism, such as one for dumping or bulldozing. Children can use trucks with simple lever mechanisms if the levers are sturdy and relatively large and have large knobs. For easy maneuverability, trucks should have large wheels.

Trains for 2-year-olds should have characteristics somewhat similar to those appropriate for younger toddlers. Older toddlers can manage trains with smaller cars and wheels, but tracks are not yet appropriate.

Transportation toys should not be too heavy for children to handle easily and should be rounded (with no sharp edges or points) and have no small, swallowable parts. Wood (if not too heavy) and plastic materials are desirable. Metal tends to be heavy and have sharp edges and is usually not appropriate for this age range.

## *Exploration and mastery play materials*

Older toddlers explore a wide variety of materials, do simple mastery activities, and begin to make constructions.

### Sand and water play materials

Sand and water play are favorite activities of older toddlers. In addition to using the play materials appropriate for younger toddlers, 2-year-olds can manage large and small tools, including sieves and strainers, and enjoy water and sand mills. Materials that can be used for fantasy play in sand or water are also appropriate for children of this age group, who are increasingly interested in pretend activities. The same safety criteria that apply to other play materials for children younger than 3 years of age also apply to sand and water materials, including the suggestion by the medical community that individual tubs be used for water play (to reduce the possibility of children spreading infection to one another).

### Construction materials

Between 2 and 3 years of age, most children begin to make constructions. Wooden unit blocks (often called kindergarten blocks) are appropriate for this age group. The basic unit is the block measuring $1^3/_8$ x $2^3/_4$ x $5^1/_2$ inches. The blocks can be hard or soft wood. Hardwood blocks are heavier, more durable, and more expensive (this expense being balanced by durability for group use). For older toddlers, sets of at least 50 to 60 blocks (per child using them at the same time) are recommended. Children of this age tend not to use the specialized forms, such as triangles and arches.

The universal appeal of unit blocks seems to lie in their relative absence of structure. The blocks are varnished rather than painted and are simple geometric forms, which allows the child to create a structure from them. These materials are open-ended in that there is no predetermined goal for their use and children are free to experiment.

Other forms of small noninterlocking blocks are generally not recommended for older toddlers. It is difficult for children this young to build stable constructions with soft, lightweight blocks, and cube blocks are not stable enough for constructing anything other than stacks or rows. On the other hand, large noninterlocking blocks (hollow wood blocks and those made of foam or heavy cardboard) are suitable for this age. In addition to playing with the interlocking blocks that younger toddlers can use (such as bristle blocks), older toddlers can press together larger (3- to 4-inch) plastic bricks, such as Duplo bricks.

Blocks and other construction materials lend themselves to many types of play, including exploration of form and shape, deliberate attempts to build something (mastery), independent fantasy activities, and dramatic play with others.

## Puzzles

Older toddlers can put together simple wood and plastic fit-in puzzles, in which one piece fits in each space. Puzzles with four or five pieces are suitable for children younger than 30 months. As children approach age 3, puzzles with 6 to 12 pieces may be used. Puzzles with knobs are easier, but the knobs should be firmly attached.

## Pattern-making materials

At around 2½ years, children begin to play with patterns, sequences, and order and begin to "create" in art activities. Although objects still slip out of their fingers, the fine motor control of children this age has improved. They can use pegboards with large pegs in a variety of colors, color cubes, color forms, and magnetic boards with animal-, human-, and geometrically shaped pieces. Pieces should not be small enough to swallow.

## Dressing, lacing, and stringing materials

Older toddlers are very interested in independence and doing things for themselves. In addition to enjoying lacing and stringing with large beads, children are interested in and will try to learn to button, snap, hook, and buckle, using frames, dressing books, or dressing dolls. They will also try to lace, using wooden lacing shoes or lacing cards (sturdy ones with large holes).

## Specific skill-development materials

By 2 years of age, children's memory span has improved so that they can remember from a previous day. They are learning to concentrate and can remember three directions at a time. They can match, grasp simple cause-and-effect relationships (e.g., turn the switch and the light goes on), and solve problems mentally. They are interested in colors and shapes and the names of things. They are eager to learn and ask many questions.

Children learn to twist beyond one turn during the third year and may begin to open keg or barrel nesting toys. They may also use simple lockbox or lock-and-key materials successfully (those with only one or two large keys that fit easily into large keyholes without complicated shapes). They may manage 5 to 10 pieces for multiple nesting and stacking activities. As they begin to recognize patterns, sequence, and order of magnitude, graduated stacking and a variety of simple sorting and matching activities are particularly interesting to them. These activities include using more complex shape sorters, color and picture dominoes, and simple lotto or other matching materials.

Older toddlers are interested in all sensory activities and can learn to discriminate between various stimuli. They are fascinated by different smells, tastes, and textures and enjoy trying to guess what they are touching in a "feel bag" (shown below) or box or what they are smelling in a "smell jar" (shown on p. 104).

## Games

Only a few board games are appropriate for older toddlers. Most 2-year-old children have developed only rudimentary problem-solving skills, such as simple matching and sorting. They are not yet capable of extended mental plans and strategies. In addition, most children in this age range are not interested in sitting and concentrating for extended periods of time. They have not left behind the period that Piaget termed the *sensorimotor stage,* when physical movement and action are of paramount importance to them. Older toddlers cannot be expected to play cooperatively with a group of other children. They do best with one other child and/or an adult.

Between 2½ and 3 years, some children enjoy simple matching or lotto games, in which the matching is based on pictures or colors rather than on more abstract concepts. Dominoes (especially giant dominoes) may also be used successfully by older 2-year-olds. In all these games, only a few matching pairs or pieces (three to five pairs) should be used. Pieces smaller than 2 inches are difficult for the child to manipulate; those between 2 and 4 inches are preferable.

## Books

Older toddlers enjoy simple stories read from picture books. They attend to short stories with repetition and/or rhymes and familiar subjects. They like stories about what they do themselves. By the age of 2½ years, they may ask questions about what is being read to them. Older toddlers prefer simple pictures with few details and bright, primary colors.

Children in this age range like looking at books individually as well as having stories read to them. They enjoy simple pop-up books and are

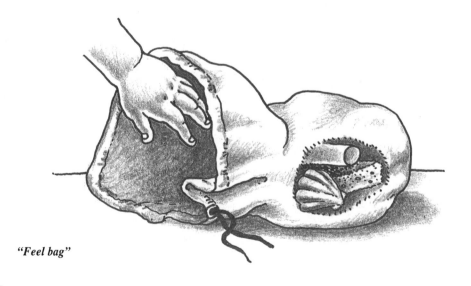

*"Feel bag"*

beginning to like "dress-me" books. They often enjoy books with pictures hidden behind movable windows or doors, although in group settings such books may easily get torn.

Books are useful for supporting social and cognitive development. As children become interested in stories, reading activities can move beyond simple labeling of objects and actions. Social interactions and feelings may be included even in very simple stories, providing models for imitation and vehicles for representation and growing understanding. To facilitate understanding, promote respect for others, and nourish the growing self-concept of older toddlers, stories and pictures should avoid stereotyped images and should reflect the diversity in the group and in the larger society. Books serve as a valuable means of broadening the experiences of children in the group.

## Music, art, and movement materials

During the third year, older toddlers enjoy using simple art materials and participate eagerly in simple rhythm, singing, and movement activities.

### Art and craft materials

Children show their first really "creative" drawings and constructions between the ages of 2 and 3 years, but it is the process of creating rather than the end product that is important to them. Thinking starts to replace acting on objects during this period. Children begin to make color distinctions and may like to paint, fingerpaint, and use Magic Markers (nontoxic and with a large point). Fine motor coordination improves a great deal over this period, and between 2 and 2½ years, the child may hold a crayon or marker using an adult grip. Children at this age may imitate *V* and *H* strokes, scribble circular strokes, and draw vertical lines. During the 2½- to 3-year period, children develop good hand and finger coordination and may move fingers independently. Many can copy circles or a cross and are beginning to be able to cut with scissors.

Appropriate materials for older toddlers include large crayons and Magic Markers; paper for drawing; fingerpaints and paper; an adjustable easel, with tempera paints, large paper, and brushes; easy-to-use blunt-ended scissors; an unbreakable chalkboard, with large chalk and an eraser; and modeling clay or dough. For safety, all materials should be nontoxic and have no sharp or pointed ends.

### Musical instruments

Older toddlers respond enthusiastically to musical and rhythm instruments. Their fine motor coordination and finger dexterity are improving, and they can now handle drums, tambourines, sand blocks, triangles, and rhythm sticks.

# Overview of Play Materials for Older Toddlers—

| Social and Fantasy Play Materials | Exploration and Mastery Play Materials |
|---|---|
| **Mirrors**<br>full-length unbreakable mirror firmly mounted or in nontippable stand<br>hand mirrors (light, sturdy, unbreakable)<br><br>**Dolls**<br>soft-bodied or washable rubber/vinyl baby dolls (12–15 inches)<br>simple accessories for caretaking—feeding, diapering, and sleeping<br>simple, removable doll clothes (closed by Velcro, large hook and loop, or snap; 12–15 inches)<br>small peg or other people figures (not swallowable) for fantasy scenes<br><br>**Role-play materials**<br>dress-up materials<br>housekeeping equipment—stove, refrigerator, ironing board and iron, telephone, pots and pans, cleaning equipment<br>simple doll equipment—bed, baby carriage (sturdy and large enough to hold child)<br><br>**Puppets**<br>small hand puppets sized to fit child's hand (that represent familiar human and animal figures and community diversity)<br><br>**Stuffed toys/play animals**<br>soft rubber, wood, or vinyl animals (6–8 inches) for exploration and pretend play<br>mother and baby animals<br><br>**Play scenes**<br>small people/animal figures, with simple supporting materials (vehicle, barn) or unit blocks to make familiar scenes<br><br>**Transportation toys**<br>small cars and vehicles to use with unit blocks (4–5 inches; sturdy wood or plastic)<br>larger vehicles for pushing and fantasy play<br>large wood trucks to ride on<br>trains with simple coupling system and no tracks (for use with unit blocks) | **Sand/water play materials**<br>people, animals, vehicles for fantasy play in sand/water<br>nesting materials useful for pouring<br>funnels, colanders, sprinklers, sand/water mills<br>small sand tools—container with shovel or scoop; rake with blunt teeth<br><br>**Construction materials**<br>wooden unit blocks (50–60 pieces)—no need for specialized forms (arches, curves)<br>large plastic bricks (2–4 inches; press-together)<br>large nuts and bolts<br><br>**Puzzles**<br>(from about 24 months)<br>4–5-piece fit-in puzzles<br><br>(from about 30 months)<br>6–12-piece fit-in puzzles (knobs make them easier to use but must be firmly attached)<br><br>**Pattern-making materials**<br>pegboards with large pegs<br>color cubes<br>magnetic boards with forms<br><br>**Dressing, lacing, stringing materials**<br>large beads for stringing<br>cards or wooden shoe for lacing<br>dressing frames and materials<br><br>**Specific skill-development materials**<br>5–10 pieces to nest/stack<br>one-turn screw-on (barrel) nesting<br>simple lock boxes<br>hidden-object pop-up boxes (with lids, doors, dials, switches, knobs)<br>safe pounding/hammering toys<br>cylinder blocks<br>shape sorters with common shapes<br>simple matching and lotto materials<br>color/picture dominoes<br>feel bag/box, smell jars<br><br>**Books**<br>sturdy books with heavy paper or cardboard pages (short, simple stories or rhymes with repetition and familiar subjects; simple, clear pictures and colors)<br>tactile/touch-me, pop-up, hidden-picture, and dressing books |

## 2 Years Old

| Music, Art, and Movement Play Materials | Gross Motor Play Materials |
|---|---|
| **Art and craft materials** <br> large, nontoxic crayons <br> large, nontoxic markers <br> adjustable easel <br> large, blunt paintbrushes <br> nontoxic paint and fingerpaint <br> large paper for drawing, painting, fingerpaints <br> colored construction paper <br> easy-to-use, blunt-ended scissors <br> chalkboard and large chalk <br><br> **Musical instruments** <br> rhythm instruments operated by shaking (bells, rattles) or banging (cymbals, drums) and more complex instruments (tambourines, sand blocks, triangles, rhythm sticks) <br><br> **Audiovisual materials** <br> adult-operated players and records, tapes, CDs, etc. <br> music with repeating rhythms—for rhythm instruments <br> music to "dance" (bounce) to <br> simple point-to and finger-play games and songs <br> short films and videos of familiar objects and activities | **Push and pull toys** <br> simple doll carriages and wagons (low, open, big enough for child to get inside) <br> push toys that look like adult equipment (vacuum cleaner, lawn mower, shopping cart) <br><br> **Balls and sports equipment** <br> balls of all shapes and sizes, especially 10–12-inch balls for kicking and throwing <br><br> **Ride-on equipment** <br> stable ride-ons propelled by pushing with feet (steering devices but no pedals; wheels spaced wide apart for stability; child's feet flat on floor when seated) <br> bouncing or rocking ride-ons (with confined rocking arc and gentle bounce for toddlers; child's feet touch floor when seated) <br><br> (as child nears age 3) <br> small tricycles (with 10-inch wheels) <br><br> **Outdoor and gym equipment** <br> tunnels <br> swings with seats curved or body shaped and made of energy-absorbing materials <br> low climbing structures and slides, with soft material underneath |

Although the four categories provide a useful classification, play materials can typically be used in more than one way and could be listed under more than one of the categories.

### Audiovisual materials

Older toddlers may learn to sing phrases of songs, often on pitch. They may try to sing along with recorded or "live" nursery rhymes and songs and like to "dance" or perform other actions to music. Movement to music may include running, galloping, swinging, swaying heads, and tapping feet. Children at this age may listen to simple recorded stories and may sit and watch a video segment of 10 minutes or so.

## *Gross motor play materials*

The older toddler's great interest in gross motor activities can be supported by safe and appropriate play materials.

### Push and pull toys

The period from age 2 to 4 or 5 years is a time of intense interest in push and pull toys that are models of objects that adults use. Toy lawn mowers, vacuum cleaners, shopping carts, baby carriages, and strollers (see also "Role-play materials," p. 70) are preferred props for pretend and role play. Most older toddlers are capable of pushing these materials without turning them over.

Although toy models that are clearly recognizable as their adult counterparts facilitate pretend play, minute detail is not necessary. Older toddlers prefer materials that make noises or have special actions, but models with these features are often too fragile for group use. For maneuverability, push toys for this age range should be low and have large wheels. For safety, edges should be rounded.

Wagons for 2-year-olds should be neither full size nor very heavy. Sturdy rounded plastic or lightweight wood wagons are appropriate and easily managed. Children are unlikely to be able to use wheelbarrows successfully before age 3, because these objects must be lifted, balanced, pushed, and steered.

### Balls and sports equipment

Older toddlers throw and retrieve all kinds of objects. They prefer (and are more successful at) playing with large balls (10 or 12 inches in diameter), which are easier for them to catch and kick than are smaller balls. With the increasing coordination of gross motor actions during this year, children are more able to focus on a target in throwing or kicking. They enjoy balls of all shapes and sizes.

### Ride-on equipment

Many of the same characteristics of ride-ons that are appropriate for young toddlers are also appropriate for 2-year-olds, although the ride-ons need not be as low or as small. Older toddlers can usually manage ride-ons that require them to bounce up and down on the seat, such as those of the bouncing-horse type with springs. Children in this age range have increased interest in what the ride-on represents. They enjoy realistic replicas of vehicles or animals but are able to pretend with less realistic, more "generic" objects as well. Many in this age range are not yet able to pedal, so tricycles are usually not appropriate. Some children as they approach age 3 can begin to manage pedals and enjoy trying to ride small tricycles (with 10-inch wheels, a wide wheel base for stability, and a depressed front bar for safety).

**OLDER TODDLERS**

### Outdoor and gym equipment

Older toddlers continue to have high interest in spatial exploration and large motor activities. New motor capacities include walking up and down stairs and jumping down a short distance. Stationary kinds of gym equipment (tunnels; low climbing structures and slides; low, safe swings) are best for children in this age range, because of toddlers' limited motor skills and poor judgment. Older toddlers are likely to get themselves to the top of a climbing structure without being able to get down. Children in this age range need constant and careful adult supervision when using outdoor and gym equipment.

## Priorities and special considerations

**Priorities** for play materials for older toddlers, 2 years of age, include providing an appropriate range of materials for their rapidly developing skills and interests. Play materials should support and nourish children's

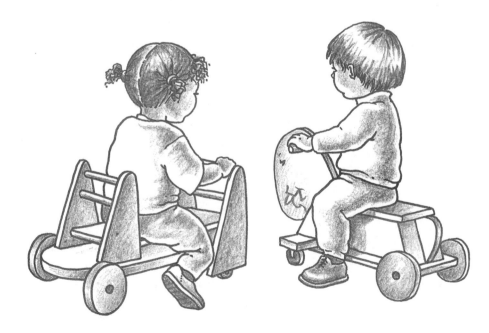

- interest in exercising increased fine and gross motor capacities;
- continuing interest in active physical play;
- growing ability to represent regularities in the environment, with accompanying interest in order and routine;
- strong preference for independence;
- increasing interest in pretend and role-play activities;
- increasing interest in social play with peers;
- growing interest in artistic expression; and
- increasing interest in problem-solving and mastery activities.

Older toddlers have a growing interest in interacting with peers and are developing social skills; their interest and persistence in their own independent activities is also increasing. Individual activities and goals may conflict with those of others. Sharing, taking turns, and playing cooperatively with others is often difficult for children in this age group. As well as becoming more aware of others, they are becoming more aware of themselves and their choices or preferences and are more likely to defend them. Providing a sufficient number and variety of materials so that children may engage in parallel play or a number of different activities can minimize friction. At the same time, including some materials and equipment that may be enjoyed by several children at once—such as a rocking boat or a heaping bowl of crayons placed in the center of the table—gently draws children out of their territoriality and gives them opportunities to enjoy social play.

Although older toddlers have greatly increased gross and fine motor skills and are interested in and capable of a wider range of activities, they still have little understanding of what might be dangerous. Their preference for independence may also lead them to try to do things by themselves that they are not yet ready to do. The play activities of older toddlers must be carefully monitored, and their play materials must still meet all the safety standards necessary for younger children. Play materials also must be regularly checked for signs of wear (chipped paint, splinters, cracks, lost pieces or parts, etc.). Careful maintenance of materials is important for safety and to provide optimal support for children's development through play. Broken or incomplete play materials can be frustrating for children and can discourage their growing interest in mastery.

**Special considerations** in group programs for older toddlers still include *health* and *cost.* As mouthing decreases and resistance to disease increases, some health concerns are reduced, but keeping materials clean is still important.

Concern about cost may increase as a greater variety of play materials is required to support children's growing capacities. Cost should be weighed against the safety and durability of materials for this and all age groups. Simple dress-ups and materials to practice dressing skills (buttoning, snapping, etc.) can be donated or sewn. Simple lotto games and matching

**OLDER TODDLERS**

## Taking Stock

### Toddlers 2 years old

Basic play materials for older toddlers:

- ❏ a full-length, unbreakable mirror
- ❏ dolls with simple garments and caretaking accessories
- ❏ role-play materials, including a selection of dress-ups; large, sturdy doll bed; child-sized stove and refrigerator; simple pots and pans; and a cleaning set
- ❏ a variety of wood, plastic, rubber, or vinyl people and animal figures to use with blocks
- ❏ vehicles (cars, trucks) to be used with blocks; a few large ride-on trucks (if cost permits)
- ❏ sand/water table(s) with containers and simple pretend materials
- ❏ a set of unit blocks and other construction materials, such as plastic bricks and large plastic nuts and bolts
- ❏ an assortment of fit-in puzzles
- ❏ pegboards with large pegs
- ❏ large beads for stringing; lacing shoes or cards with large holes; and materials to practice buttoning, snapping, buckling, etc.
- ❏ simple matching and sorting materials; graduated nesting, stacking, and ordering materials; simple lock boxes; and sensory materials, such as "feel bags"
- ❏ simple lotto games and giant dominoes
- ❏ a variety of sturdy books
- ❏ a supply of crayons, paints, paintbrushes, markers, clay or dough, scissors, chalkboard, chalk, plain and colored paper, and an adjustable easel
- ❏ a standard rhythm instrument set
- ❏ recorded music and a record, CD, or tape player
- ❏ push toys that support pretend play (vacuum cleaner, baby carriage)
- ❏ large ball(s) to kick, throw, and catch
- ❏ stable ride-on materials pushed by feet
- ❏ a low climbing structure and slide

and sorting activities can be constructed by staff or parents. Adults can also make "feel bags" by filling bags with objects of various shapes and textures and make "smell jars" by putting materials with different scents into jars. Supply budgets can be eased by making rather than buying playdough, fingerpaint, and other art supplies, using simple recipes.

Natural materials (stones, shells, pressed leaves covered with contact paper, etc.) are wonderful for sorting and matching. Household materials (funnels, unbreakable measuring cups and spoons, sturdy mixing spoons, basters, strainers, etc.) can be used for sand and water or dramatic play. Books can be made or borrowed from the library, and recycling centers can provide low-cost materials for games and art activities. These materials and household items (coffee tins with plastic tops, empty yogurt containers, etc.) can also be used to construct rhythm instruments.

Using homemade, recycled, and natural materials for play may have positive effects beyond reducing costs. It may increase children's attention to the natural world around them, help them think flexibly and creatively about materials, and increase their respect and care for the play materials prepared by teachers and parents for their use.

# Chapter 6

# Preschool and Kindergarten Children (3 through 5 years)

## Abilities and play interests _____

While children's skills and interests continue to develop and change over the years from 3 through 5, many materials are appropriate throughout this age range. Suggestions for play materials for 3- through 5-year-old children are listed together because of the large areas of overlap. An overview of typical abilities and play interests during these years—in the motor, perceptual-cognitive, and social-linguistic domains—is given below to provide a background for considering appropriate play materials. Every child will not demonstrate all of the interests and abilities mentioned. There are many individual differences in developmental rates for all children, and the development of skills and interests may vary by as much as 2 years for children in the 3-through-5 age range (not including children classified as having "developmental delays"). In addition, with increasing age, children's cultural background, family life, and individual experiences play a greater role in the development of skills and interests. To achieve an optimal match between children in the program and play materials, teachers need to take into account the previous experiences of children, as well as their current observed abilities and interests.

### *Motor*

- (by age 5) runs, jumps, climbs, and balances with assurance; gross motor skills are well developed
- likes risks, tests of physical strength and skill—typically loves acrobatics and outdoor equipment
- (as finger control increases) picks up small objects, cuts on a line with scissors, holds pencil using adult grasp, strings small beads
- builds expertly—typically loves small construction materials and also vigorous activity with unit and larger construction materials
- (by age 5) sometimes shows rudimentary interest in ball games with simple rules and scoring

### *Perceptual-cognitive*

- shows interest in senses and sensory discrimination activities (color, shape, sound, smell, taste, weight)
- shows increasing interest in simple number and quantity activities (counting, measuring, observing more/less and larger/smaller), literacy activities

(pronouncing letter names/sounds, copying letters/pretending to write, doing activities with books), and more complex matching and classifying activities

- (by age 4) engages in activities that appear more purposeful and goal directed, makes more active use of a plan
- (by age 5) sometimes sorts and matches using more than one quality at a time (e.g., color and size)
- shows increasing interest in producing designs, including puzzles, and in constructing play worlds
- engages in first representational art
- (by age 5) shows interest in product as well as process in art
- shows increasing awareness of realistic detail in models, dress-ups, dramatic play, and construction play
- shows interest in nature, science, animals, time, and how things work

## *Social-linguistic*

- shows high interest in dramatic play—re-creates adult occupations, uses costumes and props
- shows increasing interest in group pretend play
- begins to share and take turns—is learning concept of fair play
- (by age 4) engages in social play that frequently tests limits (pretend play is typically full of wild imaginings)
- (by age 5) engages in social play that is typically cooperative, practical, and conforming (pretend play uses more realistic adult roles)
- hates to lose and is not ready for organized competitive play
- enjoys simple board games based on chance, not strategy
- increasingly differentiates gender in play roles and interests
- enjoys looking at books and being read to
- (by age 5) may show interest in writing or reading words

## Initial appropriateness considerations _____

Preschool and kindergarten children have many new and improved abilities. Their improved fine motor skills increase their ability to care for themselves (buttoning and lacing) and express themselves creatively (cutting, drawing, woodworking, and building with a much larger variety of construction materials). Better developed gross motor skills allow them to use outdoor gym equipment with increasing independence and to engage in a wider variety of "sports" activities. Although children in this age group continue to enjoy practicing these skills for their own sake, they are increasingly interested in using them to pursue social and mastery goals. Activities that allow children to exercise and increase social-interaction and task-mastery skills in play are important for children's development throughout this age range.

As their representational ability expands, children's fantasy and art activities become more imaginative and creative. Interest in creating patterns with materials and drawing or constructing representations of the world also grows. Increases in language skills, control over attention, and the availability of previously learned information-processing strategies allow children to begin to solve problems mentally and plan ahead. They can successfully engage in more complex activities with people and objects.

Preschool and kindergarten children have great interest in social interaction with peers. They are becoming capable of interacting cooperatively with other children in simple games, construction and art projects, and complex dramatic play with roles and rules. They are also becoming capable of participating in organized group activities if these activities are interesting to them and not too long.

**PRESCHOOL AND KINDERGARTEN**

## Suggestions for appropriate materials _____

With their burgeoning capacities and interests, preschoolers and kindergartners enjoy many kinds of play materials, which support their social, cognitive, and physical development.

### *Social and fantasy play materials*

A variety of props and materials can support sociodramatic play, which is at its height during this period.

### Mirrors

During the preschool and kindergarten years, full-length and hand mirrors are used in fantasy and dramatic play, as well as for feedback on appearance.

### Dolls

Children in this age range can successfully manipulate dolls with articulated limbs and have increasing interest in accessories (clothes and caregiving materials) for incorporation in pretend play. By about age 5, children develop the manual dexterity to dress and undress dolls if the garments are simple and the fastenings are large. Baby dolls should fit comfortably in the child's arms. At the older end of the age range, children may be interested in dolls that look like a child their own age (especially for dressing and undressing) in addition to dolls that look like babies. Dolls should represent the range of physical and cultural differences in the children's experience. Dolls with physical or cultural features that are new to the children, such as those that represent a child with a disability, must be introduced carefully into the environment after the children have had experiences (stories, films, videos, field trips, classroom visits, etc.) that prepare them to incorporate the dolls meaningfully and positively into fantasy and dramatic play.

Fantasy play is at its height during this age period. Children of both genders use dolls that represent fantasy characters (family members, robots, police, etc.). To promote creative imaginative play, these dolls should be generic rather than detailed and specific. Action figures (super-heroes) and those representing television characters, such as Ninja Turtles and Power Rangers, are not good choices for early childhood settings because activities with the figures are typically violent and stereotyped. Fashion dolls are not well suited to the early childhood setting: they are fragile and have many small parts to be lost; they propagate stereotypical notions of beauty and place an emphasis on fashionable clothes and other possessions; and they suggest teen-age or adult role-play activities rather than activities that are appropriate for young children.

### Role-play materials

During the preschool and kindergarten years, children become capable of cooperative and dramatic play with peers. Children increasingly engage in make-believe play, acting out a variety of play themes and portraying characters very dramatically and with feeling. Gender roles often become more important in play, and boys and girls frequently focus on different themes. Typical play themes during these years include house, hospital, store, school, office, police, space, and themes from books, movies, and television programs.

Children in this age range incorporate more and more detail into their play themes and make more extensive use of props. Although they enjoy realistic equipment, they are also increasingly capable of creating elaborate settings from very simple materials. By age 4 or 5, they can create houses, offices, and schools from large blocks or cardboard boxes and can use crayons, markers, paints, and cut-out shapes to create added effects. They can use preconstructed play puppet stages and stores effectively in play but are increasingly capable of making their own stages and stores. Paradoxi-cally, children can use both more and less realistic equipment during this period. As is the case with play scenes, it may be desirable for children to construct their own play settings as they become capable of it, because this activity requires planning (often in interaction with others), mental repre-sentation, and creative effort.

In addition to enjoying the role-play materials suggested as appropriate for older toddlers, preschool and kindergarten children can use more fragile equipment, such as doll highchairs and bassinets, and more elaborate cooking, serving, and washing equipment. They benefit from a larger variety of dress-ups and props for enactment of specific roles (doctor/nurse kits, office equipment, play cameras, cash registers, play money, play food, etc.), but a number of these props can be created (in fantasy or reality) by children. Although children often are attracted by aggressive and war toys (guns, swords, and shields), these are not considered appropriate for group settings. They tend to support and foster real or pretend aggression and violence.

PRESCHOOL AND
KINDERGARTEN

## Puppets

True puppet play begins during the preschool period. Particularly by 4 years and older, children can use puppets to act out roles and simple stories or events. The easiest first puppets are sock or mitten shaped. Until the age of 5 or 6, children typically do not have the dexterity to operate puppets that have limbs. Preschool and kindergarten children can use hand, finger, and arm-and-hand puppets. They prefer soft materials and typically care little for elaborate detail on puppets as long as the facial features are clearly marked. They tend to prefer making up and acting out their own stories. They can use simple puppet theaters but do not make use of elaborate stages or scenery.

## Stuffed toys/play animals

The sturdy wood, rubber, vinyl, and plastic play animals used by younger children are also appropriate for preschool and kindergarten children. After age 3, children appreciate a larger number and variety of animals, including different varieties of fish, reptiles, dinosaurs, and other exotic animals. They are interested in learning about these animals and use them in their pretend play.

## Play scenes

The period between 3 and 6 years is a time of peak interest in creating play scenes and developing extended pretend sequences with them. Children enjoy prepackaged scenes (house, school, garage, airport, farm, zoo, etc.), but they can also construct these scenes using unit blocks or play bricks (such as Legos), with people and animal figures, vehicles, and a variety of additional props (fences, trees, road signs, barn/room enclosures, etc.). Providing materials for constructing scenes, rather than using prepackaged types, requires more flexibility and creativity on the part of the child and supports more variety in play. Children in this age range construct increasingly elaborate and detailed scenes and engage in longer and more complex play sequences with them. Several children may participate in construction and fantasy play.

### Transportation toys

Children 3 through 5 years old show great interest in play with vehicles. Although children in this age range like small, realistic metal cars and trucks (such as Matchbox brand) and small, realistic airplanes and trains with simple-to-assemble tracks, these are not usually appropriate for group settings. Vehicles such as these are relatively fragile, and their attractiveness to children can cause disputes or arouse competition for their possession. Small (3 to 4 inches) but sturdy wood or heavy plastic vehicles are useful for vehicle play in groups, with "roads" or "garages" constructed from unit blocks by children. Simple wood or plastic trains with magnetic or hook connections can also be used on simple block "tracks." In addition, children enjoy small (6- to 12-inch) or large (24- to 36-inch) wood models of trucks with sturdy working parts. Children's increasing manual skills allow them to operate more complicated mechanisms, such as large cranks. Preschool and kindergarten children typically incorporate transportation toys into fantasy and dramatic play.

## *Exploration and mastery play materials*

The rapidly expanding skills and interests of preschool and kindergarten children can be supported and encouraged by appropriate play materials.

### Sand and water play materials

Children in this age range can handle most sand and water play materials. Both large and small sand tools are appropriate, and at the older end of the age range, children can understand and manipulate sand molds. Three-through 5-year-olds actively experiment with a large variety of sand and water materials, such as cups, sieves, funnels, tubes, and water wheels. They also enjoy using fantasy materials (animals, boats, vehicles, etc.) in sand or water. Many can blow bubbles successfully without ingesting the soap.

### Construction materials

Throughout this period, block play continues to be a major play activity. Blocks are used for construction, fantasy play, and dramatic play with others. Wooden kindergarten blocks (unit blocks) continue to be appropriate and popular. A large number of blocks (at least 80 to 100 blocks per child playing at the same time) and a variety of specialized forms (such as arches and triangles) are recommended for this age group. Large plastic blocks or heavy cardboard blocks can be used, although hollow wood blocks are preferable because of their durability and stability.

Preschool and kindergarten children are able to work with most types of interlocking building systems: fitting notched logs, interlocking cogs, snapping or pressing together plastic bricks, inserting flat pieces into slots, using nuts and bolts, connecting straws, and popping tubes together.

Children of these ages are able to manipulate small bricks of less than one inch in length, although they may have difficulty taking apart small plastic bricks (such as Legos) that have been pressed together. For the more difficult coordinations, such as using a nut and bolt, the pieces should be larger (2 to 3 inches). Connecting pieces in a specific order to create models comes more easily to children older than 5.

**PRESCHOOL AND KINDERGARTEN**

## Puzzles

During the preschool and kindergarten years, children develop skill in doing puzzles and move from successfully completing 12-piece puzzles to putting together 50-piece puzzles, although there are wide individual differences. Cardboard as well as wood and plastic puzzles are now appropriate. Around age 3½ or 4 years, children can fit together large, simple jigsaw puzzles (puzzles with irregularly shaped pieces and either no frame or minimal frame support), and skill rapidly increases. Children between 3 and 6 can also fit together, and are interested in, clock puzzles and number or letter puzzles.

## Pattern-making materials

Children 3 through 5 years of age have increasing control of their fingers and have a feel for design. They exhibit order and balance in their art, building projects, and constructed play worlds. They begin to plan and create intended effects and (especially after age 5) have an increasing interest and pride in the products they produce. By age 5, children may enjoy copying designs with blocks and tiles as well as creating patterns. Throughout this age range, children continue to enjoy color cubes, color forms, magnetic form boards, and pegboards. They also can construct patterns using mosaic blocks and tiles, felt boards, plastic shapes, paper shapes and strips, and block printing equipment. By age 5, children can begin to use smaller materials (as small as ½ inch).

## Dressing, lacing, and stringing materials

Preschool and kindergarten children develop skill quickly when using materials that allow them to practice buttoning, snapping, hooking, buckling, and lacing. Most are still learning to tie bows firmly. Children of this age can use longer and thinner strings for bead stringing, but most still need a stiff tip on the string. By 4 years, a child may follow or copy a sequential pattern in bead stringing and at age 5 may string ½-inch beads successfully. Children of 3 and 4 can sew using cards, and 5-year-olds can usually manage leather or cloth and thick needles (with supervision). From age 5, children can usually manage simple weaving activities.

## Specific skill-development materials

Children 3 through 5 are increasingly goal directed in their play. Interest in creating interesting effects on the environment through exploration is somewhat replaced by interest in goal-oriented mastery, which involves creating prespecified effects. Children can now make use of a plan in their play and hold the plan in mind over time. They engage in intellectual exploration of objects, experimenting, and making simple rules. They are interested in naming and classifying the world around them and, by the age of 5, may begin to sort using more than one criterion at the same time. Most can deal with 10 or more matching or sorting pieces.

Children in this age range are interested in naming and classifying colors, shapes, numbers, letters, and natural forms (shells, stones, leaves, etc.), and they have mastered the use of spatial words and concepts, such as *back, front, under, over, in, on,* and *up.* They are interested in the physical world and enjoy exploring it with measuring and magnifying materials. They enjoy learning about their own bodies and taking care of plants and animals. By age 5, children may also like to practice copying and naming letters, counting objects and matching them to numerals, and comparing sizes of objects.

A large variety of specific skill-development materials are appropriate for 3- through 5-year-old children. Materials should be selected that support the development of a broad range of skills, but, to be effective, they must be integrated with program goals and be used in ways designed to help children reach these goals. The availability of materials alone is not enough to support or promote development. Adults must relate them to ongoing interests and activities in the program and help children use the materials appropriately and effectively. Generic materials that can be useful in programs for 3- through 5-year-old children include

- materials for matching, sorting, or ordering (by color, shape, size, texture, smell, taste, picture, number, letter, or concept);
- complex lock boxes, including those that require keys or several steps to open;
- geometric concept materials, including simple puzzles with shapes divided into fractions (halves, thirds, fourths, etc.);
- simple counting and number materials (objects to count, order, and match to numbers);
- measuring materials, including balance scales (shown on p. 115), trundle wheels (shown on p. 93), and unbreakable thermometers;
- counting or see-through clocks;
- simple models of mechanical devices (pendulum, gears, levers), plant parts, body parts or bones, etc.;
- materials for simple science experiments—color-mixing materials, color paddles, unbreakable prisms, sink-and-float objects, unbreakable magnifying glasses of different strengths, large-screen microscope, stethoscope, etc.;
- specimen collections (rocks, shells, leaves);
- plants and animals to care for and habitats (ant farm, aquarium); and

• print materials, such as large-size print sets and simple, working
typewriters.

Specific materials in each of these categories can be introduced as
children's skills and interests prepare them to use the materials effectively
and as program planning and development makes them relevant. Adult
guidance, monitoring, and support is needed for children's optimal use and
benefit from almost any play material.

A number of beginning computer activities become appropriate
during these years. Computer hardware and software are big invest-
ments for early childhood programs. Not only do program staff need to
consider a great many technical and educational factors in making
selections but the technology and software on the market change
rapidly. For these reasons, this book does not address the area of computers. The Resources section (p. 125) lists several publications that
offer guidance in using computers effectively with young children and
in selecting computer hardware and software.

## Games

After age 3, many types of sit-down games become appropriate. During
the preschool and kindergarten period, children develop longer attention
spans, the ability to take turns in a game and follow a simple plan of action
(i.e., moving a piece from start to finish), and interest in acquiring basic
knowledge about numbers and letters. These developments pave the way
for simple game activities. Favorite games for these children, especially at

the lower end of this age range, depend on chance rather than on strategy or skill, because most preschool children have not yet developed the mental operations required to formulate a consistent, long-term strategy (holding several sequences of moves in mind at the same time and weighing alternatives). Games should be simple, with few rules and simple scoring systems.

Matching and lotto games continue to be appropriate, as do dominoes. In addition, games requiring simple fine motor coordination (such as balancing pieces on top of each other) can often be used successfully. For the older end of this age range, matching games can be based on simple letters and numbers as well as on pictures and colors. Games based on number recognition (1 to 10) may be enjoyed by children from about age 5. Some simple card games based on matching and visual memory (such as Concentration) may be successfully used by 5-year-olds. Younger children usually do not have the manual dexterity to hold and manipulate cards and may have trouble keeping track of many cards. For 3- and 4-year-olds, games with spinners may be easier than those involving dice. Simple race games are appropriate, in which the child only has to move a piece along a preordained path. Children younger than 6 or 7 are typically not able to take into account another's game piece as well as their own, so games should not require "blocking" an opponent. Children's inability to tolerate losing (once they understand that there is such a thing) is also an important consideration in choosing or adapting games for them.

## Books

Children in this age range enjoy looking at books and love having adults read to them. They may sit for 20 minutes or longer to hear stories, but extended reading to small, interested groups is more effective than trying to hold the attention of large numbers of children for long periods of time. Preschool and kindergarten children continue to enjoy familiar subjects but like more details and less repetition than at earlier ages. There are large differences in the quality of books available for this (and every) age range. Librarians specializing in materials for children and special publications reviewing children's books can help in selecting books with lasting quality.

Three-year-old children may insist on stories being told and retold, word for word, without changes. They may respond to questions about stories and typically like to comment. They are constantly asking "why." Most 3-year-olds enjoy stories about children their own age, the here and now, and animals (especially animals that act like people). They often like books about adventures with familiar things, such as telephones or trucks, to help them assimilate their own experiences. They also enjoy information books about everyday life experiences (in the firehouse, the zoo, the city, the country). Children of this age also like books with humor and incongruity, word and alphabet books, and books with rhymes.

Four-year-olds love ridiculous and silly stories and wild, dramatic, and fantastic stories. They typically delight in jokes, humorous stories, nonsense rhymes, and tall tales. They enjoy fantasy, although they are still in the process of learning to distinguish fantasy from reality and fact from fiction in children's books. Like younger children, children in this age group like animal books, verse, and stories about everyday life. Some like factual books. Most enjoy complex illustrations with an abundance of detail. They also like to make up their own stories and enjoy making books with the help of adults. Many (especially boys) are fascinated by somewhat violent stories containing death (of monsters, for instance), killing, and objects that crash, fall down, or break. Most 4-year-old children like to hear and create stories with silly language and plays on words.

**PRESCHOOL AND KINDERGARTEN**

Five-year-olds often show preferences for certain stories, which they like to hear over and over. They usually love to be read to and may memorize their favorite stories and act them out with their friends. They also make up stories to act out. Children of this age are typically interested in new words and are continually asking their meaning. They may be interested in trying to read simple, early reading books. Although 5-year-olds still enjoy a fairy tale or other fantasy-based story, they become increasingly interested in credible stories with "here-and-now" themes. They often like poetry, holiday and seasonal stories, and stories about animals who behave like human beings. They are able to understand and enjoy books with words and pictures in "comic strip" style (words in balloon frames spoken by pictured figures) and may try to interpret these books on their own.

## *Music, art, and movement materials*

The developing skill and imagination of children in this age range support interest in a wide variety of music, art, and movement activities and in the creative use of appropriate materials.

### Art and craft materials

Art and craft interests and skills develop rapidly over the years in this age range. At about age 3, children learn to handle scissors, can use paste to make a collage, and have improved control of crayons and pencils. They may draw thin lines and copy a simple shape, such as a circle. They add a few body parts to an outline figure of a person. Their drawing is typically not representational, and they are still more interested in process than product in art.

At about age 4, children may begin to do some representational drawing and may make a person figure. They may be able to copy a few more simple figures and add several body parts or features to an outline human form. By this age, many children can copy a pattern in bead stringing, thread small beads for a necklace, and cut on a line with scissors. They are becoming more interested in the products of their artistic efforts and show pride in them.

By age 5, children may do more elaborate representational drawings, and their drawings are more realistic. A 5-year-old's drawing of a house may have a door, windows, a chimney, and a roof. They often say what they will draw before beginning and are becoming more critical of their work. Children of this age can usually hold a pencil, brush, or crayon in an adult-style grasp. They can copy a wide variety of figures, and many begin trying to write letters or numbers. They can usually use scissors skillfully and weave simple designs.

Materials appropriate for 3- to 5-year-old children include

- crayons, markers, and colored pencils (large crayons and markers until age 5);
- finger and tempera paints;
- an adjustable easel;
- brushes of varying sizes;
- paper of varying sizes and colors;
- scissors with rounded ends;
- paste and glue;
- materials for collages and three-dimensional constructions;
- modeling clay or dough and tools;
- chalkboards and chalks of varying sizes;
- block printing equipment; and
- a workbench with a vise, hammer, nails, and saw.

By age 5, children can use watercolor paints and smaller drawing and painting materials.

## Musical instruments

Children's musical skill increases dramatically during these years. In addition to displaying improvements in singing and dancing ability, they enjoy experimenting with rhythm instruments and playing them with other children in groups. They can also play a wider variety of instruments, including castanets and xylophones. Preschool and kindergarten children can blow into and produce sounds from instruments such as harmonicas, ocarinas, various horns, and simple recorders. For sanitary reasons, blowing instruments should be washable or used by only one child.

## Audiovisual materials

During the preschool and kindergarten years, children show a great increase of skill and interest in audiovisual activities. They respond to music with increasing skill. At age 3, they gallop, jump, and run, keeping time with the music fairly well. Their movements become more graceful and varied until by about age 5 they are doing real dancing. At 3, they remember the words of many songs and continue to enjoy playing rhythm instruments or dancing to recorded or live music.

Four-year-olds can usually play simple singing games (following a live or recorded lead), and many show an increase in voice control. They can recognize and sing whole songs, very often singing on pitch. They have great interest in dramatic songs and often create songs in play. They love to move to music and may give dramatic performances.

By age 5, children may recite or sing rhymes and jingles as well as songs. Many enjoy the mastery of melodies and tunes and may sing well. They can work together and follow the beat of music. They can act out a story in dance form and like to dress up while dancing. They love recorded music and can manage, by themselves, audiovisual equipment designed for children. They often like to record their own voices and music on blank tapes.

Children in this age range also enjoy a variety of educational films and videotapes, including stories about children and animals and simple factual presentations about the lives, activities, and habitats of animals and children.

## *Gross motor play materials*

As gross motor skills develop, children are able to safely and successfully use a wider range of play materials.

### Push and pull toys

Push and pull toys continue to interest children through a good part of this period. As children's motor coordination increases, they become capable of successfully using wagons and wheelbarrows, as well as the simple push toys that represent adult tools (lawn mowers, vacuum cleaners, etc.). Preschoolers notice and are interested in tools that look like their real counterparts, although with increasing representational ability they do not need this level of realism for pretend play. By about age 5, children prefer tools that really work (e.g., sweepers that really clean), but they play just as well with props that do not work—and even with props that are generic and flexible in appearance. By the end of this age range, interest in push and pull toys has declined. One exception is the full-size wagon, which children continue to use throughout the early childhood period.

### Balls and sports equipment

Three-year-olds begin to show interest in a variety of catch-and-throw games. Many are able to kick a ball hard, catch a large ball, and throw underhand. However, they do not have the coordination or the interest to play group or team ball games with competition and rules.

# Overview of Play Materials for Preschool and Kindergarten

## Social and Fantasy Play Materials

### Mirrors

full-length (upright), unbreakable mirror, firmly mounted or in nontippable stand

hand mirrors (light, sturdy, unbreakable)

### Dolls

washable rubber/vinyl baby dolls (with culturally relevant features and skin tones)

accessories (culturally relevant) for care-taking—feeding, diapering, and sleeping

smaller people figures for use with blocks and play scenes

(from age 5)

child-proportioned dolls (with features and skin tones representing different races)

simple doll clothes (closed by Velcro, large hook and loop, or snap or buttons; culturally relevant)

### Role-play materials

dress-up materials (more culturally relevant roles and more details)

role-relevant props—cash register, doctor materials, office materials

housekeeping equipment—stove, refrigerator, ironing board and iron, telephone, pots and pans, flatware, serving dishes, cleaning equipment

doll equipment—bed, baby carriage, stroller, highchair

### Puppets

small hand/arm/finger puppets (sized to fit children) that represent familiar and fantasy figures

simple puppet theater (no scenery)—older children can construct one

### Stuffed toys/play animals

rubber, wood, or vinyl animals (4–8 inches)—for pretend play with blocks and to provide replicas of real animals for learning

domestic (farm), wild (zoo), and sea animals, reptiles, and dinosaurs

### Play scenes

small people/animal figures

supporting materials—vehicles, road signs, barn—for use with blocks or other materials to make familiar scenes (favorite scenes include house, farm, garage, airport, space, fort)

### Transportation toys

cars and vehicles to use with unit blocks (3–4 inches, sturdy wood or plastic)

larger vehicles, with simple working parts, to push and to use in fantasy play

large wood trucks to ride on

small trains with magnetic or hook connections and simple wood tracks (unit blocks can be used for tracks)

## Exploration and Mastery Play Materials

### Sand/water play materials

tubs for sand/water play (perhaps individual tubs for water play)

people, animals, vehicles for fantasy play in sand/water

measures, funnels, strainers, tubes, sand/water mills

large and small sand tools

(from age 4)

sand molds, water pump

### Construction materials

wooden unit blocks (80–100 pieces per child playing), including specialized forms (arches, curves)

large hollow blocks

plastic bricks (2–4 inches; press-together type)

(from age 4)

most types of interlocking blocks except metal or smaller than ½ inch

### Puzzles

fit-in or framed puzzles:

    age 3—up to 20 pieces

    age 4—20–30 pieces

    age 5—up to 50 pieces

large, simple jigsaw puzzles (10–25 pieces)

number and letter puzzles, puzzle clocks

cardboard puzzles

### Pattern-making materials

pegboards with smaller pegs

color cubes

magnetic boards with forms

(from age 4)

variety of shapes/colors/sizes of beads for patterned stringing

mosaic blocks, felt boards

(from age 5)

smaller beads for stringing (½ inch by age 5)

block printing materials

### Dressing, lacing, stringing materials

cards, wooden shoe for lacing

dressing frames and materials

simple sewing cards

(from age 5)

beginning weaving materials

### Specific skill-development materials

materials for matching, sorting, and ordering (by color, shape, size, texture, smell, taste, picture, number, letter, or other category concepts, such as "fruits" or "insects")

geometrical concept materials, including simple shape and fraction materials

simple, concrete number materials (for counting and matching to numerals)

measuring materials—balance scales, graded cups for liquid, etc.

simple mechanical devices—gears, levers

science materials—prism, magnifying glass, color paddles, stethoscope

natural materials—rocks, shells, seeds—to sort

plants and animals to care for

printmaking materials—shapes, letters, numbers

beginning computer software/hardware

### Games

dominoes (color, picture)

simple matching and lotto games (color, picture)

bingo (color, picture)

(from age 4)

simple card games (such as Concentration-type memory games)

games requiring simple fine motor coordination (picking up or balancing objects)

# Children—3 through 5 Years

| | Music, Art, and Movement Play Materials | Gross Motor Play Materials |
|---|---|---|

first board games (based on chance, not strategy; with few rules; simple scoring)

(from age 5)

dominoes based on number

bingo/lotto based on letter or number matching

## Books

picture books, simple stories, rhymes (abundance of detail in illustrations)

complex pop-up books

(common age-3 interests)

here-and-now stories

animal stories

alphabet picture books

words and rhymes

(common age-4 interests)

wild stories, silly humor

nonsense stories/rhymes

information books

(common age-5 interests)

realistic stories

animals that behave like people

poetry

simple early reading books

---

## Art and craft materials

large nontoxic crayons (many colors)

large nontoxic markers (many colors)

adjustable easel

paintbrushes of various sizes

nontoxic paint and fingerpaint

large paper for drawing, painting, fingerpainting

chalkboard and large chalk

colored construction paper

easy-to-use, round-ended scissors

paste and glue

collage materials

clay/dough and tools

(from age 4)

workbench (hammer, saw, nails)

(from age 5)

smaller crayons/markers

watercolor paints

simple sewing forms with large, blunt needles

## Musical instruments

all rhythm instruments, including castanets and xylophones

blowing instruments—horn harmonica, recorder (for one-child use only, for sanitary reasons)

## Audiovisual materials

Live (typically piano) music is also appropriate where recorded music is recommended

recorded music for singing

recorded music for movement, including dancing and pretend character activities

recorded music to use with rhythm instruments (see "Musical instruments" above)

recorded music, songs, rhymes, and stories for listening

short, high-quality films and videos, such as those that show animals in their natural environment

---

## Push and pull toys

small wagons and wheelbarrows

push materials that look like adult equipment (vacuum cleaner, lawn mower, shopping cart)

(from age 5)

full-size wagons, scooters

sweepers that really work

## Balls and sports equipment

balls of all shapes and sizes, especially 10–12-inch balls for kicking and throwing

(from age 4)

lightweight (hollow plastic) softball and large, lightweight bat (with constant supervision)

(from age 5)

jump rope

lightweight flying disk

## Ride-on equipment

tricycles sized to child

3- and 4-wheeled pedal toys

vehicles with steering mechanism

full-size rocking/bouncing "horse"

ride-ons that several children can use together

(from age 4)

low-slung tricycles

## Outdoor and gym equipment

soft surface under all gym equipment at all ages

stationary outdoor climbing equipment

swings with seats curved or body shaped and made of energy-absorbing materials (but children at this age do not pump legs, so they have to be pushed)

(from age 4)

slides with side rails and ladders

ropes, hanging bars, and rings on swing or climbing equipment

outdoor building materials

---

Although the four categories provide a useful classification, play materials can typically be used in more than one way and could be listed under more than one of the categories.

Some 4-year-olds enjoy striking a ball with a bat. The first baseball bat should be lightweight (a large, plastic version), and the ball should be soft. Ball and bat activities can be dangerous, especially in group settings. If these materials are provided, children need constant, careful supervision by an adult.

Five-year-olds have more adequate catching, throwing, and kicking skills and may begin to show rudimentary interest in games with simple rules and scoring. Kickball, soccer, and baseball are typical interests, although the process of doing the activity interests the child more than sticking to rules and competing in an organized way. Structured team games with competing sides are not yet appropriate. Five-year-olds may also begin to be able to use jumpropes and throw flying plastic disks, especially light ones.

## Ride-on equipment

Early in this age range, most children learn to pedal, which opens the door for all sorts of 3- and 4-wheeled pedal vehicles. The children like realistic ride-ons (cars, trucks, horses, etc.), but these items may not be practical or desirable for group play. Sturdy, realistic ride-ons typically are very expensive, and competition for their use may generate disputes. In addition, realistic appearance may limit play value, because it is difficult to use a real-looking truck for a car or a fire engine. More generic ride-on toys have more flexibility in fantasy play.

Tricycles should be sized to the child: 12- to 13-inch wheels are usually the right size for 3- and 4-year-olds. At around 4 or 5 years, children begin to be able to maneuver scooters and low-slung tricycles.

## Outdoor and gym equipment

The 3-year-old is still in the process of developing good gross motor coordination. By age 4, gross motor coordination is much better; children can run, jump, and climb with assurance; pump a swing; climb a rope ladder; and climb up an inclined board. Along with possessing increased motor skills, the 4-year-old has a new interest in testing these skills with a variety of physical feats (swinging very high, jumping from heights, hanging upside down). Starting around 4 to 5 years, children are interested in acrobatics.

Age 4 or 5 years is the time for all kinds of climbing structures, especially ones with many movable parts (swings, ropes, hanging bars, and rings). Children also like climbing structures with potential for imaginative, role-playing activities. For instance, climbing structures with walled enclosures are wonderful props for fantasy play.

Children in this age range (especially 3- and 4-year-olds) have immature judgment. They are not yet able to foresee all of the consequences of their actions and may do dangerous things with the equipment. This lack of judgment, coupled with children's love of physical testing and unorthodox use of gym equipment, means that all use of outdoor and gym equipment must be carefully monitored by adults.

## Priorities and special considerations

**PRESCHOOL AND KINDERGARTEN**

**Priorities** to be considered when choosing play materials for 3- through 5-year-old children include

- taking into account the wide range of abilities and interests that children bring to the program because of developmental and environmental (economic, sociocultural) differences;
- supporting and nourishing growing interest and skill in peer interaction (as shown in children's dramatic play activities; cooperation and joint effort in construction, games, and tasks; and participation in group activities);
- providing for children's increasing capacity for artistic expression (in arts and crafts, music, and movement);
- encouraging the development of children's intrinsic motivation to understand and be effective in the world (by supporting curiosity, experimentation, persistence, and successful mastery of skills and tasks);
- promoting the development of children's perceptual and representational skills;
- helping children develop effective learning and social-interaction strategies; and
- providing information that increases children's understanding and interest in learning about a topic.

Play materials for this age range should be planned to support an increasingly broad spectrum of abilities and interests. As children grow older, their skills and interests are shaped by previous experiences to a great extent. Although experiences in the group setting will further shape children's interests and abilities, programs must start by meeting children where they are—by matching their existing skills and interests.

As children become more interested in peers during this period, they benefit from materials that support positive, cooperative interaction and minimize disputes and negative (hostile, violent, rejecting) interaction. In addition to having appropriate materials, children need many opportunities to engage in social interaction. They also need adult guidance to prevent problems and support for cooperatively resolving the problems that do occur. Providing materials for creative and cooperative dramatic play (as well as for other forms of cooperative social interaction) that allow a variety of uses and evolve as children's interests and abilities evolve is an important part of supporting social development in this age range.

To support their intrinsic motivation and the development of independent learning strategies, children need materials that allow them to experiment, discover, and succeed with a minimum of adult intervention. Providing play materials in many domains (art, construction, nature, science and health, language and literacy, spatial and numerical relations) promotes children's broad-based perceptual and conceptual development and supports children's growing understanding and interest. Materials in any of these domains can also support the development of process skills, such as matching, ordering, and classifying.

The Taking Stock checklist on page 103 suggests specific types of materials that should be represented in programs for 3- through 5-year-old children. The list is basic rather than exhaustive and does not include all materials that are appropriate for this age range.

Although children in this age range are less likely than are younger children to put materials in their mouths, careful maintenance remains important for safety and to retain optimal play value. Materials should be regularly checked for signs of wear (chipped paint, splinters, cracks, or lost pieces). Children find broken or incomplete play materials frustrating and are not encouraged to take good care of materials.

**Special considerations** in selecting play materials for group programs for 3- through 5-year-old children include controlling *costs* while providing a range of materials with sufficient *variety and levels of challenge* to meet the needs of all the children in the group.

As at every age, cost should be weighed against the safety, durability, and play value of the materials. Increasing numbers of materials for this age range can be made by parents, teachers, and the children themselves. Dress-ups can be made or salvaged from clean used clothing. Parent contributions may be especially helpful in providing culturally appropriate dress-up materials. Homemade materials for matching, sorting, and ordering may be provided by parents, teachers, and children. Sensory discrimination materials (such as feel bags, shown on p. 74, and smell jars, shown on p. 104) may be homemade, and graded-color materials can be made from nontoxic house paint samples. Modeling dough and fingerpaint can also be homemade.

An increasing variety of natural materials (rocks, shells, leaves, seeds, pressed flowers, and sterilized bones (saved from meals or found in natural settings) are wonderful for matching, sorting, and ordering. A larger variety of household materials (funnels, unbreakable measuring cups and spoons, mixing spoons, small rolling pins, cookie cutters, basters, sifters, strainers, etc.) can be used for experiments, sand and water play, or dramatic play. Parent contributions can be especially useful because parents can supply examples of household materials particular to different cultural traditions. Books can be made or borrowed from the library, and recycling centers can provide numerous low-cost materials for games and art activities. These materials and household items (such as sturdy tins with no sharp edges and empty cartons and containers) can be used to make games, instruments, and three-dimensional art constructions.

**PRESCHOOL AND KINDERGARTEN**

## Taking Stock

### Children 3 through 5 years old

Basic play materials for preschool and kindergarten children:

- ❏ a full-length, unbreakable mirror mounted on a wall or in a sturdy stand
- ❏ dolls of various ethnicities, including those of the children in the program, with clothes and caregiving accessories (e.g., bottles, blankets)
- ❏ a variety of dress-ups (with increasing levels of role-relevant details) and supporting props for various themes
- ❏ a variety of hand puppets
- ❏ materials for constructing play scenes, including blocks and human and animal figures
- ❏ a variety of sturdy vehicles for use with blocks
- ❏ sand and water play materials for exploration and experimentation (measures, strainers, tubes, funnels) and materials for fantasy play in sand and water
- ❏ construction materials, including large and small unit blocks, large hollow blocks, and a variety of other small materials for construction
- ❏ a variety of puzzles (fit-in, framed, jigsaw), with the number of pieces appropriate to children's ages
- ❏ beads for stringing (size depends on age); pegboards; pattern-making materials (pattern blocks and tiles, weaving materials) for the older end of the age range
- ❏ dressing, lacing, and stringing materials to learn simple self-help skills and beginning sewing activities

## Taking Stock, cont'd

### Children 3 through 5 years old

- ❏ specific skill-development materials that include activities related to matching, sorting, and ordering by shape, color, letter, number, etc.; equipment related to science and the natural world
- ❏ a variety of games, e.g., dominoes, lotto, simple card games, bingo, first board games (with the outcome based on chance, not strategy)
- ❏ a large variety of books appropriate to the ages, interests, and experiences of the group
- ❏ a large variety of art and craft materials, including both graphic and plastic materials
- ❏ a standard rhythm instrument set (and instruments such as wood xylophones if cost permits)
- ❏ recorded music (and player) for singing, moving, and playing rhythm instruments
- ❏ push and pull toys that support sociodramatic play (wagon, doll carriage, vacuum cleaner)
- ❏ a variety of balls for specific sports activities, such as kicking, throwing, and catching (beanbags can also be used for throwing and catching; target games for the older end of the age range)
- ❏ pedal tricycles (appropriate for children's size and age)
- ❏ outdoor and gym equipment (e.g., climbing gym, swings, slides, ladders, seesaw by age 5) proportioned to children's size and capabilities; also sand and gardening tools and all-weather construction equipment

As noted in Chapter 5, using homemade, recycled, and natural materials for play may have positive effects beyond reducing costs. It may increase children's attention to the natural world, help them think flexibly and creatively about materials, and increase their respect and care for the play materials prepared by teachers, parents, and their peers for their use. Including child-made materials may also increase children's self-esteem and feelings of responsibility for and control over their environment.

With the rapid expansion and diversification of children's skills and interests over this age range, providing sufficient variety and levels of complexity and difficulty for all children in the group becomes increasingly important and challenging. One way of accommodating widening ranges of preference and ability is to provide materials that can be used in a number of different ways and at different levels of complexity or difficulty. Blocks, well-designed construction materials, and balls are good examples of flexible, open-ended materials. Many art and pattern-making materials can be used by children with widely varying interests, fine motor skills, and levels of representational development. Materials for matching, sorting, and ordering also allow flexibility, because children can use different numbers of pieces (of the same material) or different criteria for matching, sorting, or ordering. The most useful commercially available beginning games for this age group are designed to be played in different ways, depending on children's conceptual level.

To support and nourish the development of children from a variety of cultural and economic backgrounds, the environment must contain materials that have elements that are familiar and connect with children's experiences, as well as novel materials that expand children's horizons. Social and fantasy play materials should include props that allow children to represent and extend their understanding of objects and events in their everyday lives as well as to explore new roles.

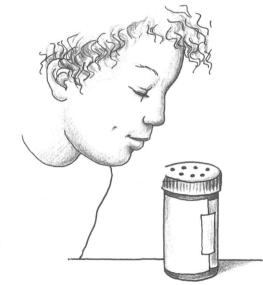

*"Smell jar"*

Exploration and mastery materials can also arouse children's interest by meeting them on familiar ground. Books with familiar scenes and situations can help children represent and mentally manipulate the familiar in new ways that may enhance sensitivity and deepen understanding. Books can also expand children's imagination and vocabulary and help them think about experiences they have never had. Pictured objects in games, puzzles, matching activities, and other similar activities can also include familiar and culturally relevant themes to support interest and understanding. Criteria for sorting and rules in games can also take culture and experience into account.

**PRESCHOOL AND KINDERGARTEN**

Music, art, and movement materials can accommodate cultural differences. Art objects from different cultural traditions can be displayed in the environment, and materials for creating similar objects can be provided. Songs and music for listening, dancing/moving, and using with instruments can include appropriate, culturally relevant material. Rhythm instruments used in different cultures can also be included. Simple films and videotapes showing the lives of children in different environments and cultures can also be useful if the topics and level of the presentations are appropriate for the interests and conceptual levels of the children.

Careful observation of children as they interact with play materials, as well as communication with children and parents, can help caregivers in selecting play materials with an appropriate variety and range of levels for the children in the group.

# Chapter 7

# Primary-School Children (6 through 8 years)

## Abilities and play interests

Beginning school does not signal the end of children's need for "play" in learning. Concrete experiences are the basis of learning throughout early childhood, and play continues to be important for supporting and nourishing both cognitive and social development during the school years. An overview of typical abilities and play interests over the primary school years—in the motor, perceptual-cognitive, and social-linguistic domains—is given below to provide a background for considering appropriate play materials.

As is the case with younger children, every child will not demonstrate all of the interests and abilities mentioned. There are individual differences in developmental rates for all children, and the development of particular skills and interests may vary by two years or more for children from 6 through 8 years of age. Differences in learning style may also become apparent. Methods and materials that are useful for one child may not be as useful for another. In addition, individual interests and preferences become more apparent during this period.

The relative influence of culture and past experience on children's skills and interests also increases as they grow older. This may be especially noticeable as children become more self-conscious and as peer influences play a greater role in their development. To meet the needs and support the development of primary-school children, teachers must take into account the children's previous experiences, as well as their current observed abilities and interests, when selecting play and learning materials and planning for their use.

### *Motor*

- engages in a variety of large muscle activities, including jump rope, hopscotch, stunts, and climbing (trees, trapeze), ice skating, roller skating, bicycle riding, water sports, ball play
- engages in a variety of small muscle activities, including printing, drawing and tracing with pencils, simple sewing, simple carpentry, weaving, braiding, stringing small beads, cutting out detailed shapes (such as paper dolls), assembling jigsaw puzzles with many pieces
- is motivated to practice in target games or to improve a skill

## Perceptual-cognitive

- is able to direct attention voluntarily and to maintain a focus for increasingly extended periods
- enjoys challenges that test developing skills (as long as these challenges can be successfully met)
- enjoys reading, spelling, and printing activities and games
- shows interest in simple arithmetic activities and games and in time, calendars, weights, and the value of coins
- shows interest in nature and simple science activities and experiments
- enjoys hobbies and collecting things
- likes to produce finished products (through art, models, crafts, sewing, carpentry)
- shows interest in the line between fantasy and reality—likes magic and "tricks"
- begins to show interest in other times and other places

## Social-linguistic

- shows much interest in the peer group and in "belonging"—enjoys special friends, cliques, gangs, secret languages and passwords
- generally prefers playing with same-gender peers
- displays increasing ability to play cooperatively with others—enjoys group activities
- shows interest in "fair play" and living up to standards (own and group's), but cannot yet bear to lose in games and may become very upset or "cheat" to win
- continues to enjoy dramatic play (puppets, dolls, paper dolls, dress-ups, attack-and-defense themes: police, cowboy, military, space); increasingly interested in producing shows and plays
- begins to show interest in the wider community (beyond the immediate neighborhood and familiar experiences)

# Initial appropriateness considerations _____

Children in this age range benefit from a number of the types of materials that support and nourish development in earlier years, as well as additional, more complex play and learning materials. Materials that facilitate social understanding and cooperative interaction continue to be important and can be expanded to include concepts in social studies. Children are increasingly peer oriented during these years and are better able to consciously cooperate, negotiate with each other, and

stick to simple rules in games. They are also more apt to form groups that exclude others as they learn to use and create rules and strategies for social acceptance and successful interaction. Antibias materials and those that promote responsibility, respect for others, and cooperation may help to reduce these tendencies.

Materials that support creative expression in art, music, and movement also continue to be important. Many children develop an interest in formal lessons in one or more of the arts during this period, and some schools offer beginning group or individual instruction. Opportunities for creative self-expression can nourish awareness, sensitivity, and confidence. They can also provide another area for skill development and achievement for children in the early school years, who are now more interested in products and outcomes and more aware of their own relative performance.

An increasing variety of materials are useful and important for promoting the development of literacy, mathematical and spatial understanding, mechanical understanding, concepts related to nature and science, critical thinking, and understanding of the "scientific method." Well-designed materials can also support the development of "process" skills, which help children learn how to learn. Process skills include multiple and hierarchical classification, measuring, graphing, sequencing, planning, monitoring and correcting performance, hypothesis generation and testing, and logical inference.

Providing children the opportunity to choose and carry out learning activities independently supports the development of persistence, effective self-direction, and intrinsic motivation. Providing a variety of materials for children's independent learning activities (alone or with peers) is one dimension of effectively responding to individual differences in the classroom. When children have available a variety of materials at different levels of challenge and in a variety of interest areas, they can participate in a curriculum that meets their individual needs.

## Suggestions for appropriate materials

Including a variety of appropriate materials for play and learning in the primary classroom allows children more choice and independence in their learning activities.

### Social and fantasy play materials

Primary-school children's developing ability to create models of the world around them and engage in planned cooperative activities can be supported by the provision of appropriate materials.

## Mirrors

By about 6 years, children are self-conscious and self-aware and use mirrors in much the same way as adults—to check the image of the self that is presented to the world.

## Dolls

At the beginning of this age range, children's doll play still focuses primarily on playing house with baby dolls. Lifelike baby and child dolls with many clothes and accessories are preferred for detailed role-play activities. Doll and housekeeping activities may be most useful for younger primary-school children. As children develop a preference for collections of dolls (character dolls, action figures, teenage dolls, or other model figures) and detailed realistic assessories rather than sociodramatic play in groups, doll-play activities become less appropriate in the school setting. Even children in third grade or higher, however, incorporate small human figures into detailed representations of their own fantasy scenes and models related to curriculum themes (a Native American village, a house in ancient Egypt, a river or rain-forest scene, etc.).

## Role-play materials

Role-play equipment that helps children create and act out real-life experiences (store, library, post office) can be especially useful. Props such as cash registers that add and subtract; play money in real denominations (children can create things to sell); book cataloging and check-out systems for classroom books; materials for writing, sorting, and "sending" letters; and many other "real-life" materials that can be integrated into classroom activities provide valuable learning experiences in ways that are interesting to children. Culturally diverse role-play materials, introduced in a way that enables their meaningful use, can help build social understanding and respect for others.

At the upper end of this age range, children especially enjoy giving plays and shows. They love costumes, props, and make-up or disguise materials. Having children create costumes and props themselves may provide more meaningful and lasting learning experiences. Primary-school children also enjoy using real equipment for cooking or sewing for special projects.

## Puppets

During the early school years, especially as they approach age 8, children become more concerned about the details of puppets and puppet shows, such as the characters' facial expressions, costumes, refinements of movement, props, and scenery. Costumes, props, and scenery can be made by children, who can even learn to make the puppets themselves. At about age 8, children become capable of operating puppets with arms and jointed figures that require more manipulation and action (but not marionettes yet). Puppets with hard heads and painted faces are typically preferred to the soft puppets used by younger children, but soft puppets that allow a variety of interesting manipulations are still appropriate.

Among 6- and 7-year-olds, puppet play tends to consist of acting out and replaying familiar stories. Around age 8, children often become interested in acting out scripted puppet plays with props. Although children enjoy character puppets (representing familiar figures in stories), these puppets are expensive, and children can create costumes and props for more generic models to make them look like the figures desired for the story or play. Children may use puppets for role play when they become too self-conscious for dramatic play. They can use puppets to act out a number of social issues and themes and as a vehicle for incorporating and learning about cultural differences. Books that describe ways of making and using puppets for this age range are useful; a few are included in the selected bibliography.

### Stuffed toys/play animals

For this age range, play animals provided for use in school settings are typically incorporated into constructed scenes or models or used as representations of animals to be studied.

### Play scenes

Interest in constructing fantasy worlds continues through ages 6 or 7, then may start to decline. Although they love realistic detail, primary-school children can create very realistic scenes by combining generic construction materials with small human and animal figures and filling in with art materials. They may even be able to create whole scenes with art materials (such as "beautiful junk"). Children often work together to create these scenes, and their production supports the development of representational skills, flexible thinking, and creativity. These projects may continue over days or weeks.

### Transportation toys

School-age children continue to be interested in small, collectable vehicles, but these items are usually not practical for use in school settings. Simple representations of vehicles may be used in scenes or models. Children may also be interested in trying to construct vehicles either at the workbench or with small construction materials.

## Exploration and mastery play/learning materials

A variety of concrete materials can support primary-school children's interest in understanding the wider world and purposefully practicing and mastering new skills and concepts.

## Sand and water play materials

At this age, children enjoy experimenting with and creating models using sand and water together. These activities are often incorporated in science and social studies activities, with children making models of real and fantasy scenes, such as dams, rivers, lakes and islands or other land and water forms, and habitats. Representations of plants, human and animal figures, and houses or other buildings are often included in the scenes. Small, individual tubs or larger tubs for group projects can be used.

## Construction materials

Construction materials continue to provide rich opportunities for developing cooperative social skills, visual representation, and spatial and mechanical understanding. They can also be used to create scenes and models. School-age children still enjoy building with wooden blocks, often building complex structures and models with realistic detail. Because they like to construct and use these structures over extended periods of time, teachers and staff should try to ensure that the structures can be preserved for reasonable periods. Many children now prefer construction sets with interlocking pieces, with which they can produce realistic, detailed models. They are able to use tiny screws, nuts, and bolts and all-metal parts.

## Puzzles

From about 6 years of age, children can fit together three-dimensional puzzles and models of increasing complexity. Children's puzzle skill steadily increases to approximately the adult level at about age 10. There are wide individual differences among children, but jigsaw puzzles of 50 to 100 pieces are usually considered suitable for primary-school children. Children may enjoy working on complex puzzles together (groups of two or three).

## Pattern-making materials

Primary-school children continue to enjoy designing with blocks and tiles, but they are more interested in producing a material result than in exploring or experimenting with materials. Children in this age range enjoy art materials that allow them to create permanent designs with a variety of materials (paper, wood, plastic, cardboard, beads, ceramic tiles, cloth, etc.).

## Dressing, lacing, and stringing materials

Primary-school children have mastered dressing (they may learn to tie bows by age 5 or 6) and are moving from simple stringing and lacing to simple crafts. They can string beads of almost any size and can use needles (with careful monitoring) to do so. They can also use pottery or glass beads or other more fragile materials. They are now interested in

using their skills to construct products such as jewelry or bead designs. Many children can spool knit, braid, and use more elaborate weaving devices, and some children show interest in making clothes for puppets or dolls. Such activities can now be incorporated into art and craft projects or special instruction in the arts, although children's skill levels and interest vary. Staff comfort with and competence in a craft area is important for incorporating it successfully into group settings.

## Specific skill-development materials

Primary-school children show interest in and benefit from a number of specific skill-development materials. They work at reading and writing, enjoy picking out letters on a typewriter or computer keyboard, and like to make their own books. They can use more complex printing sets, with punctuation marks to make sentences. They also show interest in using the computer to write (and read and practice spelling).

Children in this age range also show interest in experimenting with numbers, counting, and measuring and want to be able to tell time and understand money. There are a huge variety of math manipulables available that are useful for 6-, 7-, and 8-year-olds. Many manipulables support mathematical understanding by providing concrete examples of simple and more complex numerical concepts, which children can discover through experimentation. Many materials provide concrete representations of arithmetic and geometric sequences and patterns and allow children the excitement of discovering these regularities independently. Children often are fascinated by materials representing fractions and geometric relationships, which can help them develop a firm basis for understanding numerical and spatial relationships. They are able to use simple measuring instruments, such as scales (platform, balance, spring), rulers, tape measures, trundle wheels (shown on p. 93), and liquid measures, with some precision.

*Platform, balance, and spring scales*

Primary-school children enjoy materials related to clocks and "buying" things with play money (that represents denominations used in real life). During this period, children may also enjoy experimenting with simple calculators and using computer programs that teach numerical and spatial concepts.

Children in this age range are interested in their own anatomy and in the wider world around them. They can use all of the science materials recommended for preschool and kindergarten children, plus more complex equipment. They may enjoy microscopes, especially the large-screen variety that can be viewed by several children at a time, and may be interested in making and viewing slides. They are interested in telescopes, field binoculars, equipment for simple weather observations, materials for simple chemical experiments, and models of the solar system, the moon, and other features of the heavens.

A number of more complex computer programs can be used in primary school. There are text-revealing, narrative, interactive-fiction, and story-writing programs designed for this age group, as well as a few telecommunications programs and databases. Some programs teach typing skills, and there are an increasing number of simple word-processing and desktop-publishing programs. Simple computer-education programs (of the "Logo" type) introduce the child to computer programming. In addition, there are problem-solving, drill-and-practice, draw/paint, graphics-construction, graphing, spreadsheet, and music-making programs. Many programs allow several children to work together collaboratively. Books are now available that describe computer programs for children in some detail. Some of these books provide critical reviews of the program's quality and relevance for different ages (see Resources on p. 125).

## Games

Interest in games builds during this age period. For 6- and 7-year-olds, games must still be relatively simple and straightforward, with few rules and little skill or strategy required. At these ages, children may still not be able to concentrate and remember rules and strategies for extended periods. At about age 8, however, children have achieved a number of skills that pave the way for increased interest in games. Children are becoming capable of consciously formulating and carrying out a plan or strategy. They are also becoming capable of true cooperative interaction in game situations and have typically developed an interest in competition. In addition, improved reading skills allow them to read and understand game directions and board markings on their own.

In addition to the simple board and card games recommended for younger children, this age range can play simple word games (as they learn to read and spell) and number games. They can play simple trading games, card games, guessing or deductive games, and beginning strategy games (checkers, Chinese checkers). They are also capable of more complex memory games, such as Trivial Pursuit, requiring recall of simple facts. Primary-school children often enjoy games based on fantasy or adventure themes. Their motor coordination has developed sufficiently to allow them to master games requiring aiming (such as marbles) or balancing their bodies in different positions (such as pretending to be statues).

**PRIMARY SCHOOL**

Children at the older end of this age range may enjoy creating and constructing games, which can be placed in the classroom and shared with others.

### Books

During the primary-school years, children learn to read with increasing fluency, and most enjoy being read to. They also develop very individual reading habits and preferences. There are a number of reference guides to children's literature that can help in selecting appropriate books for this age range. Books written by children in the class can make wonderful additions to classroom book areas and have positive effects on self-esteem and motivation.

## *Music, art, and movement materials*

A variety of materials can support primary-school children's developing self-awareness and their interest in acquiring a new skill and producing a product.

### Art and craft materials

The art and craft activities of 6-, 7-, and 8-year-olds begin to make a transition toward the more adult-like arts and crafts of 9- to 12-year-olds. Primary-school children continue to enjoy many of the activities of younger children, such as drawing, painting, pasting, and modeling with

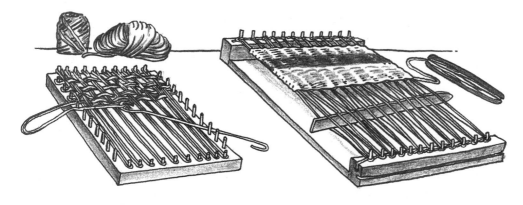

*Looper and heddle looms*

clay, but their efforts become more and more skilled, and the products produced look more finished. Children may become more interested in sewing and woodworking and enjoy being introduced to other crafts, such as leatherwork, papier-mâché, enameling, and model building (as well as the weaving, braiding, spool knitting, and small-bead stringing noted under "Dressing, lacing, and stringing materials" on p. 114). Some begin to enjoy photography, but this activity is rarely available in school art programs.

By age 6, children sometimes like to draw using colored pencils, as well as crayons and markers. They are able to cut and glue more elaborate figures and enjoy using tape. They may be able to sew (by hand) with cloth, using large stitches. By about age 7, both boys and girls may be able to sew a straight line and enjoy sewing activities, and they may attempt increasingly complex weaving, coloring, cutting, and woodworking designs. Many 8-year-olds use perspective in drawing and are able to produce wood products.

Many art and craft materials are appropriate for this age range. Children can use more sophisticated coloring materials of all kinds (crayons, markers, colored pencils, art chalks, pastels, and paints, including watercolors). As they focus more on products, children show more interest in using sketch pads (and all art papers), stencils, regular scissors, and pastes and glues of all kinds (dangerous kinds should be avoided). They are interested in clay that hardens into a permanent shape and simple pottery activities. Looper and heddle looms (shown on p. 117), more complex printing equipment, and a more complete woodworking tool set (to be used with constant supervision) may be introduced. For special projects and models, children can successfully use plaster of paris, papier-mâché, leather sewing and braiding materials, and small-bead stringing materials (for jewelry, decorations, etc.).

## Musical instruments

During the primary-school years, children can begin to learn to play real instruments and to read music. From the age of 7 or 8, some show interest in formal lessons (piano, autoharp, recorder, flute, violin, guitar, horn, etc.). Recorders are frequently used in group music instruction in schools for this age range. A wider variety of instruments for children to explore can be borrowed from or brought in by parents or musicians who visit as special guests. These instruments are most useful when their range of sound and proper use and handling can be demonstrated and questions can be answered by someone who knows the instruments well.

## Audiovisual materials

Over this period, children may grow in skill and interest in singing, playing instruments, and moving to music. They are increasingly able to perform together and take "parts" in a group. Many can now replicate a tune accurately and match a rhythm for playing or dancing, and they can use their own songbooks. By age 8, many children like group folk singing and folk dancing with established movements and patterns.

Children in this age range can use some audiovisual materials in the classroom by themselves. They may enjoy listening for long periods to stories, songs, and instrumental music (typically with earphones with multiple jacks, in a group setting). They may also like to record their own reading, reciting, singing, and instrument playing so that they can play it back.

**PRIMARY SCHOOL**

## Gross motor play materials

An expanding number of gross motor materials can support primary-school children's increased ability to participate in games with rules and their interest in acquiring new skills.

### Balls and sports equipment

During this period, children may begin to enjoy playing on teams, but adults should take care not to emphasize competition. Primary-school children can understand and enjoy games with rules. Six- and 7-year-olds are still developing the coordination necessary for skilled participation in sports. By age 8, children may be interested in ball games (kickball, baseball, soccer, basketball, etc.), skating and hockey (although few school programs have these activities available), and target games like horseshoes. Six- and 7-year-olds usually do better with junior- or child-size sports equipment. By 8 years, children may be able to manage and have a preference for regular, or adult, versions.

### Ride-on equipment

Most children learn to ride a bicycle without training wheels at about 6 years of age, and by age 7 few are interested in tricycles. Primary-school children may show much interest in bike riding, but bicycles typically are not included in group (school) settings. (For safety, the appropriate size of a bicycle depends on the size of the child. Particularly on a male-frame bike, the child should be able to straddle the bike with both feet on the ground. By age 7 or 8 years, children can safely operate hand as well as foot brakes on bicycles.)

### Outdoor and gym equipment

Young primary-school children love climbing in general and acrobatics in particular. This is also the prime age for tree climbing. The complex climbing structures described for 4- and 5-year-olds are also appropriate for 6- and 7-year-old children. After about age 8, interest in this type of outdoor gym equipment typically decreases, partly because children become too large for the equipment and partly because they are becoming more interested in sports equipment.

# Overview of Play Materials for Primary-School Children—

| Social and Fantasy Play Materials | Exploration and Mastery Play Materials |
|---|---|

**Social and Fantasy Play Materials**

**Mirrors**

same as for adult use

**Dolls**

washable, rubber/vinyl baby dolls (with culturally relevant features and skin tones) (for younger children—age 6)

accessories (culturally relevant) for caretaking—feeding, diapering, and sleeping (for younger children—age 6)

smaller people figures for use with blocks or construction materials (for fantasy scenes and models)

**Role-play materials**

materials for creating and practicing real-life activities—play money with correct denominations, book- and letter-creating materials

**Puppets**

puppets that represent familiar and fantasy figures for acting out stories (children can also create their own)

simple puppet theater—children can construct one (children can create props and scenery)

**Stuffed toys/play animals**

realistic rubber, wood, or vinyl animals to incorporate into scenes and models or that show characteristics of animals being studied (such as reptiles and dinosaurs)

**Play scenes**

small people/animal figures and supporting materials with which to construct fantasy scenes or models related to curriculum themes

**Transportation toys**

small, exact (metal) replicas preferred by children of this age range are not usually used in school settings, but more generic small models are useful

construction or workbench materials for children to use to make models of forms of transportation

**Exploration and Mastery Play Materials**

**Construction materials**

a large number of varied materials for detailed construction and for creating models (can use metal parts and tiny nuts and bolts)

**Puzzles**

three-dimensional puzzles

jigsaw puzzles (50 to 100 pieces)

**Pattern-making materials**

mosaic tiles, geometric puzzles

materials for creating permanent designs (art and craft materials)

**Dressing, lacing, stringing materials**

bead-stringing, braiding, weaving, spool-knitting, and sewing materials now used in arts and crafts

**Specific skill-development materials**

printing materials, typewriters, materials for making books

math manipulatives, fraction and geometric materials

measuring materials—balance scales, rulers, graded cups for liquids, etc.

science materials—prism, magnifying materials, stethoscope

natural materials to examine and classify

plants and animals to study and care for

computer programs for language arts, number, and concept development and for problem-solving activities

**Games**

simple card and board games

word games, reading and spelling games

guessing games

memory games (Concentration)

number and counting games (dominoes, Parcheesi)

beginning strategy games (checkers, Chinese checkers)

**Books**

books at a variety of difficulty levels for children to read

storybooks for reading aloud

poetry, rhymes, humorous books, adventure books, myths

books made by children

# 6 through 8 Years

| Music, Art, and Movement Play Materials | Gross Motor Play Materials |
|---|---|
| **Art and craft materials**<br><br>a large variety of crayons, markers, colored pencils, art chalks, and pastels (many colors)<br><br>paintbrushes of various sizes<br><br>a variety of paints, including watercolors<br><br>a variety of art papers for drawing, tracing, painting<br><br>regular scissors<br><br>pastes and glues (nontoxic)<br><br>collage materials<br><br>clay that hardens<br><br>tools (including pottery wheels)<br><br>more complex printing equipment<br><br>craft materials, such as simple looms, leather for sewing and braiding, papier-mâché, plaster of paris, small beads for jewelry making, etc.<br><br>a workbench with more tools and wood for projects (with careful supervision)<br><br>**Musical instruments**<br><br>real instruments, such as recorders (sometimes used for group lessons in school settings)<br><br>a wider range of instruments for children to explore (borrowed or brought in by parents or special guests)<br><br>**Audiovisual materials**<br><br>music for singing<br><br>music for movement, including dancing (folk dancing by age 8)<br><br>music, singing, rhymes, and stories for listening<br><br>audiovisual materials that children can use independently | **Balls and sports equipment**<br><br>youth- or standard-size balls and equipment for beginning team play (kickball, baseball, etc.)<br><br>materials for target activities (to practice skills)<br><br>**Ride-on equipment**<br><br>(children may be very interested in riding bicycles, but this is no longer included as a school activity)<br><br>**Outdoor and gym equipment**<br><br>complex climbing structures, such as those appropriate for age 5 (including ropes, ladders, hanging bars, rings) |

Although the four categories provide a useful classification, play materials can typically be used in more than one way and could be listed under more than one of the categories.

# Priorities and special considerations _____

**Priorities** to be considered when choosing materials for primary-school children include

- taking into account the increasingly wide range of abilities and interests that children bring to the classroom because of developmental and environmental (economic, sociocultural) differences;

- providing materials that encourage respect for individuals with differing backgrounds, interests, and abilities;

- supporting children's growing ability to cooperate and participate in cooperative learning activities with others;

- providing materials in a variety of domains (including art, music, and movement) so that children have multiple ways to discover and express their skills;

- supporting children's growing sense of competence by providing materials at appropriate levels of challenge for their developing skills;

- encouraging children's intrinsic motivation to understand their environments and attain competence in dealing with their physical and social worlds by providing materials that support individual interests, expand curiosity and experimentation, and allow independent decision making and problem solving; and

- promoting the development of effective learning strategies by providing materials and activities that permit the discovery or creation of organizing principles, generation and testing of hypotheses, and creation of sequences of planned problem-solving activities.

Play and learning materials for this age range should be planned to support and stimulate an increasingly broad spectrum of abilities and interests. Children have more distinct preferences than they did at earlier ages and may more clearly demonstrate individual learning styles. Culture and past experience have played a major role in developing these preferences and styles, and the peer group has begun to exert a significant influence on children's interests.

Materials that engage children in joint projects and games can promote cooperative interaction and respect for the different contributions that individuals with different skills can make. Children learn negotiation strategies in cooperative groups, and many games help them develop representational skills and higher-level strategies.

Providing a large variety of skill-building materials, in a number of interest areas and at a number of difficulty levels, helps to individualize the curriculum in a way that optimizes individual progress. A range of well-chosen materials helps children develop interest in different areas, and being able to use these materials independently supports children's feelings of self-confidence and intrinsic motivation. Because children are concrete

## Taking Stock

### Children 6 through 8 years old

Basic play and learning materials for primary-school children:

❏ small figures that may be used in fantasy scenes and constructed models

❏ materials for enacting real-life activities (buying and selling, checking out books, sending letters), and materials (to make props and costumes) for plays and performances (role-play materials)

❏ a variety of puppets provided or made by children (characters appropriate to children in the group)—to replay familiar stories and give performances and shows

❏ a variety of materials for constructing play scenes and models—to be used with blocks or construction materials (ages 6 and 7)

❏ a large variety of construction materials, which may include unit blocks and may be used to build scenes and models

❏ a variety of puzzles (jigsaw, three-dimensional), including 50- to 100-piece jig-saws, map puzzles

❏ a large variety of specific skill-development materials, including printing and book-making materials, math manipulatives, measuring equipment, materials for learning about money and telling time, science materials (including those related to weather, the solar system, plant and animal life, and basic human anatomy), and computer programs

## Taking Stock, cont'd

### Children 6 through 8 years old

❏ complex pattern-making materials (mosaic tiles, geometric puzzles) to develop spatial, mathematical, and artistic understanding

❏ a variety of games to develop interaction skills, planning, using strategies, and an understanding of rule systems—simple reading, spelling, and math games; guessing or deductive games; memory games; simple card games; and beginning strategy games (games may be created by the children)

❏ a large variety of books appropriate to the ages, interests, and experiences of the group, including books made by children in the group

❏ a large variety of art and craft materials, including both graphic and malleable materials appropriate for practicing skills and producing products

❏ recorded music for group singing, moving, and rhythm activities, and equipment for listening and recording

❏ a variety of balls and equipment for specific sports activities, such as kickball, and materials for simple target games

❏ complex outdoor and gym equipment (may include climbing gym, swings, slides, ladders, seesaw), especially for ages 6 and 7, for acrobatics

thinkers at these ages, activity with objects is still important, and appropriate materials enable them to achieve deeper understanding of concepts.

The Taking Stock list on page 123 contains general types of materials that are particularly useful in programs for primary-school children. The list is basic rather than exhaustive and does not include all materials appropriate for children in this age range.

Careful maintenance of materials remains important for this age range. Materials that are broken or have missing pieces are frustrating and provide less-effective support for learning and discovery.

**Special considerations** in selecting play and learning materials for primary-school children continue to include controlling *costs* while providing a range of materials with sufficient *variety and levels of challenge* to meet the needs of all the children in the group. In addition, materials must support development in the *specific curriculum areas* considered important in primary education (reading and language arts, mathematics, science, and social studies).

Although many kinds of materials that support learning in this age range may be purchased, increasing numbers of materials can also be made by teachers and children. Because children at this age can use fragile paper and cardboard materials, the teacher can design manipulatives and games to meet specific interests and needs. Children can make books, games, puppets, props for scenes and shows, and their own costumes and scenery.

Generic materials, such as counting cubes, can be used in a large variety of ways and with children at many different ability levels. Materials, including paper, from recycling centers can also be used for counting activities, as well as art projects and model building. Libraries can provide old or surplus books, and children can make their own.

Natural materials to support and extend science interests can be brought from home or discovered on field trips. Seeds and everyday fruits and vegetables can also form the basis for a variety of science activities. Science and children's museums sometimes lend materials appropriate for science or social studies and provide interesting field trips, in any case.

Children are able to express their interests more clearly by these ages, which makes it easier for teachers to notice these interests and build on them. Materials that expose children to new areas of exploration can be especially successful when introduced at these ages, because children are curious and eager to learn about the wider world around them.

All of the basic curriculum areas can be addressed in integrated ways at these ages, with materials and activities that interest children and provide avenues for their expanding curiosity and growing desire to extend and prove their skills.

# Resources

Abrams, B.W., & N.A. Kauffman. 1990. *Toys for early childhood development: Selection guidelines for infants, toddlers, and preschoolers.* West Nyack, NY: The Center for Applied Research in Education.

Gives examples of specific toy products and suggests ways in which toys might be used with children of different ages.

Bredekamp, S., & T. Rosegrant, eds. 1992. *Reaching potentials: Appropriate curriculum and assessment for young children.* Vol. 1. Washington, DC: NAEYC.

Suggests guidelines for appropriate curriculum for children ages 3 through 8 years.

Bullough, R.V., & L.F. Beatty. 1991. *Classroom applications of microcomputers.* 2d ed. New York: Merrill/Macmillan.

Provides basic information about varieties of equipment used in classrooms and examples of types of software available.

Clements, D. 1985. *Computers in early and primary education.* Englewood Cliffs, NJ: Prentice Hall.

A resource for using computers with young children, including software in different curriculum areas and guidelines for setting up computers and choosing software.

Cullinan, B.E. 1989. *Literature and the child.* 2d ed. San Diego, CA: Harcourt Brace Jovanovich.

Discusses usefulness of different varieties of literature in the classroom, outlines possible classroom activities, and suggests books for different interests and age groups from infancy through elementary school.

Derman-Sparks, L., & the A.B.C. Task Force. 1989. *Anti-bias curriculum: Tools for empowering young children.* Washington, DC: NAEYC.

Gives suggestions for helping both staff and children respect each other as individuals and eliminate barriers based on race, culture, gender, or ability.

Frost, J.L. 1992. *Play and playscapes.* Albany, NY: Delmar.

Contains detailed descriptions of playground equipment and innovative outdoor environments for young children.

Jambor, T., & S.D. Palmer. 1991. *Playground safety manual.* Birmingham, AL: American Academy of Pediatrics.

Serves as a practical guide to promoting playground safety, with checklists and resources for planning.

Lekotek. n.d. *Lekotek play guide for children with special needs,* and Lekotek. n.d. *Play is a child's world: A Lekotek resource guide on play for children with disabilities for family, friends, and professionals.* Evanston, IL: National Lekotek Center.

The National Lekotek Center (1-800-366-PLAY) is the administrative and training center for a nationwide network of 51 Lekotek centers, toy lending libraries, and resource centers that provide support, information, and toys to families with children who have special needs.

Oppenheim, J., & S. Oppenheim. 1993. *The best toys, books and videos for kids: The 1994 guide to 1,000+ kid-tested, classic and new products for ages 0–10.* New York: Harper-Collins, HarperPerennial.

U.S. Consumer Product Safety Commission. 1986. *Which toy for which child: A consumer's guide for selecting suitable toys—Ages birth through five.* Washington, DC: Author.

U.S. Consumer Product Safety Commission. 1986. *Which toy for which child: A consumer's guide for selecting suitable toys—Ages six through twelve.* Washington, DC: Author.

Van Hoorn, J., P. Nourot, B. Scales, & K. Alward. 1993. *Play at the center of the curriculum.* New York: Merrill/Macmillan.

Discusses specific types of play materials in relation to a play-centered curriculum and includes a chapter on play with computers.

Wolery, M., & J.S. Wilbers, eds. 1994. *Including children with special needs in early childhood programs.* Washington, DC: NAEYC.

Contains information on a variety of issues related to inclusion and includes a chapter on designing inclusive environments for young children with special needs, with emphasis on physical space and materials.

Wright, J.L., & D.D. Shade, eds. 1994. *Young children: Active learners in a technological age.* Washington, DC: NAEYC.

Contains discussions of how to integrate computers into programs for young children and suggestions for useful programs.

# Selected bibliography

Allen, K.E., & L. Marotz. *Developmental profiles: Pre-birth through eight.* 2d ed. Albany, NY: Delmar, 1994.

Ames, L.B., & C.C. Haber. *Your seven year old.* New York: Dell, 1987.

Ames, L.B., & C.C. Haber. *Your eight year old.* New York: Dell, 1989.

Ames, L.B., & F.L. Ilg. *Your four year old.* New York: Dell, 1976.

Ames, L.B., & F.L. Ilg. *Your five year old.* New York: Dell, 1979.

Ames, L.B., & F.L. Ilg. *Your six year old.* New York: Dell, 1979.

Ames, L.B., & F.L. Ilg. *Your two year old.* New York: Dell, 1980.

Ames, L.B., & F.L. Ilg. *Your three year old.* New York: Dell, 1985.

Ames, L.B., F.L. Ilg, & C.C. Haber. *Your one year old.* New York: Delacorte, 1982.

Bergen, D., ed. *Play as a medium for learning and development: A handbook of theory and practice.* Portsmouth, NH: Heinemann, 1988.

Bloch, M, & A.D. Pellegrini, eds. *The ecological context of children's play.* Norwalk, CT: Ablex, 1992.

Block, J., & N. King, eds. *School play.* New York: Garland, 1987.

Borstelmann, L.J. Children before psychology. In *Handbook of child psychology,* ed. P.H. Mussen. New York: John Wiley & Sons, 1983.

Bredekamp, S., & T. Rosegrant, eds. *Reaching potentials: Appropriate curriculum and assessment for young children.* Vol. 1. Washington, DC: NAEYC, 1992.

Bretherton, I. *Symbolic play: A development of social understanding.* Orlando, FL: Academic, 1984.

Bronfenbrenner, U. *Two worlds of childhood: U.S. and U.S.S.R.* New York: Simon & Schuster, 1972.

Bruner, J.S. The nature and uses of immaturity. In *Play: Its role in development and evolution,* eds. J.S. Bruner, A. Jolly, & K. Sylva. New York: Basic, 1976.

Bruner, J.S., A. Jolly, & K. Sylva, eds. *Play: Its role in development and evolution.* New York: Basic, 1976.

Burtt, K.G., & K. Kalkstein. *Smart toys.* New York: Harper Colophon, 1981.

Campbell, P.F., & G.G. Fein, eds. *Young children and microcomputers.* Englewood Cliffs, NJ: Prentice Hall, 1986.

Canadian Toy Testing Council. *The toy report 1985.* Ottawa, Ontario, Canada: Tyrell, 1985.

Caplan, F. *The second twelve months of life.* New York: Bantam, 1978.

Caplan, F. *The first twelve months of life.* New York: Bantam, 1980.

Caplan, T., & F. Caplan. *The power of play.* Garden City, NY: Anchor, 1970.

Caplan, T., & F. Caplan. *The early childhood years.* New York: Perigee, 1983.

Clements, D.H. *Computers in early and primary education.* Englewood Cliffs, NJ: Prentice Hall, 1985.

Consumer Guide, ed. *The complete baby book.* New York: Simon and Schuster, 1979.

Copple, C., I. Sigel, & R. Saunders. *Educating the young thinker: Classroom strategies for cognitive growth.* Hillsdale, NJ: Erlbaum, 1984.

Duckworth, E. *"The Having of Wonderful Ideas" and other essays on teaching and learning.* New York: Teachers College Press, 1987.

Eibl-Eibesfeldt, I. *Ethology: The biology of behavior.* New York: Holt, Rinehart & Winston, 1970.

Ellis, M. Play and the origin of species. In *Play as a medium for learning and development,* ed. D. Bergen. Portsmouth, NH: Heinemann, 1988.

Evans, J., & P. Stewart. *Toys: More than trifles for play. A review of the toy industry, educational claims, safety standards and precautions, toy selection and toy libraries.* Austin, TX: Southwest Educational Development Lab, 1980.

Fein, G.G. Pretend play in childhood: An integrative review. *Child Development* 52 (1981): 1095–118.

Fein, G.G., & M. Rivkin, eds. *The young child at play: Reviews of research.* Vol. 4. Washington, DC: NAEYC, 1986.

Froebel, F. *The education of man.* New York: D. Appleton, 1975.

Frost, J.L., & B.L. Klein. *Children's play and playgrounds.* Boston: Allyn & Bacon, 1979.

Frost, J.L., & S. Sunderland, eds. *When children play.* Wheaton, MD: Association for Childhood Education International, 1985.

Furby, L., & M. Wilke. Some characteristics of infants' preferred toys. *Journal of Genetic Psychology* 140 (1982): 207–19.

Garvey, C. *Play: The developing child.* Cambridge, MA: Harvard University Press, 1990.

Gesell, A., F.L. Ilg, & L.B. Ames. *The child from five to ten.* Rev. ed. New York: Harper & Row, 1977.

Gottfried, A.W., & C.C. Brown, eds. *Play interactions: The contributions of play materials and parental involvement to children's development.* Lexington, MA: D.C. Heath, 1986.

Hartley, R.E., & R.M. Goldenson. *Complete book of children's play.* Rev. ed. New York: Thomas Y. Crowell, 1970.

Hartley, R.E., L. Frank, & R. Goldenson. *Understanding children's play.* New York: Teachers College Press, 1952.

Herron, R.E., & B. Sutton-Smith. *Child's play.* New York: John Wiley & Sons, 1971.

Hill, D.M. *Mud, sand, and water.* Washington, DC: NAEYC, 1977.

Hirsch, E.S., ed. *The block book.* Washington, DC: NAEYC, 1984.

Hughes, F.P. *Children, play, and development.* Boston: Allyn & Bacon, 1991.

Isenberg, J.P., & J.E. Jacobs. *Playthings as learning tools.* New York: Wiley, 1982.

Jambor, T., & S.D. Palmer. *Playground safety manual.* Birmingham, AL: American Academy of Pediatrics, 1991.

Jenkins, P.D. *The magic of puppetry: A guide for those working with young children.* Englewood Cliffs, NJ: Prentice Hall, 1981.

Johnson, D.M. *Children's toys and books: Choosing the best for all ages from infancy to adolescence.* New York: Charles Scribner's Sons, 1982.

Johnson, J.E. The role of play in cognitive development. In *Children's play and learning: Perspectives and policy implications,* eds. E. Klugman & S. Smilansky. New York: Teachers College Press, 1990.

Johnson, J.E., J.F. Christie, & T.D. Yawkey. *Play and early childhood development.* Glenview, IL: Scott, Foresman, 1987.

Jones, S. *Good things for babies.* Boston: Houghton Mifflin, 1976.

Kaban, B. *Choosing toys for children: From birth to five.* New York: Schocken, 1979.

Kelly-Byrne, D. *A child's play life: An ethnographic study.* New York: Teachers College Press, 1989.

Klugman, E., & S. Smilansky, eds. *Children's play and learning: Perspectives and policy implications.* New York: Teachers College Press, 1990.

Leach, P. *Your baby and child from birth to age five.* New York: Alfred A. Knopf, 1993.

Lederman, E. *Educational toys and games: A practical guide to selection and utilization.* Springfield, IL: Charles C. Thomas, 1987.

Mann, B.L. Effects of realistic and unrealistic props on symbolic play. In *Child's play: Developmental and applied,* eds. T.D. Yawkey & A.D. Pellegrini, 359–76. Hillsdale, NJ: Erlbaum, 1984.

Matterson, E.M. *Play and playthings for the preschool child.* New York: Penguin, 1965.

McCall, R.B. Exploratory manipulation and play in the human infant. *Monographs of the Society for Research in Child Development* 39 (Serial No. 155), 1974.

McLoyd, V.C. Scaffolds or shackles? The role of toys in preschool children's pretend play. In *The young child at play: Reviews of research.* Vol. 4, eds. G. Fein & M. Rivkin. Washington, DC: NAEYC, 1986.

Mergen, B. *Play and playthings: A reference guide.* Westport, CT: Greenwood, 1982.

Monighan-Nourot, P., B. Scales, J. Van Hoorn, & M. Almy. *Looking at children's play: A bridge between theory and practice.* New York: Teachers College Press, 1987.

Montessori, M. *The Montessori method.* New York: Schocken, 1964.

National Toy Library Association & Play Matters. *1985 good toy guide.* London: A & C Black, 1985.

Piaget, J. *Play, dreams, and imitation in childhood.* New York: Norton, 1962.

Piaget, J. *The origins of intelligence in children.* New York: Norton, 1963.

Pulanski, M.A.S. Toys and imaginative play. In *The child's world of make-believe: Experimental studies of imaginative play,* ed. J.L. Singer. New York: Academic, 1973.

Rogers, C.S., & J.K. Sawyers. *Play in the lives of children.* Washington, DC: NAEYC, 1988.

Ruben, K.H., ed. *Children's play.* San Francisco: Jossey-Bass, 1980.

Rubin, K.H., & N. Howe. Toys and play behaviors: An overview. *Topics in Early Childhood Special Education* 5: 1–9, 1985.

Rubin, K.H., G.G. Fein, & B. Vandenberg. Play. In *Handbook of child psychology.* Vol. IV, ed. E.M. Hetherington, 693–774. New York: John Wiley & Sons, 1983.

Ruff, H.A. Infants manipulative exploration of objects: Effects of age and object characteristics. *Developmental Psychology* 20 (1984): 9–20.

Salk, L. *Your child's first year.* New York: Simon & Schuster, 1983.

Saul, W., & A.R. Newman. *Science fair: An illustrated guide and catalogue of toys, books, and activities for kids.* New York: Harper & Row, 1986.

Seefeldt, C. *The early childhood curriculum: A review of current research.* New York: Teachers College Press, 1987.

Singer, D.G., & J.L. Singer. *The house of make-believe: Play and the developing imagination.* Cambridge, MA: Harvard University Press, 1990.

Singer, J., ed. *The child's world of make believe.* New York: Academic, 1973.

Smilansky, S. *The effects of sociodramatic play on disadvantaged preschool children.* New York: John Wiley & Sons, 1968.

Smilansky, S. Sociodramatic play: Its relevance to behavior and achievement in school. In *Children's play and learning: Perspectives and policy implications,* eds. E. Klugman & S. Smilansky. New York: Teachers College Press, 1990.

Smilansky, S., J. Hagan, & H. Lewis. *Clay in the classroom: Helping children develop cognitive and affective skills for learning.* New York: Teachers College Press, 1989.

Smith, P.K., ed. *Play in animals and humans.* Oxford, UK: Basil Blackwell, 1984.

Sutton-Smith, B. Children's play: Some sources of play theorizing. In *Children's play,* ed. K.H. Rubin. San Francisco: Jossey-Bass, 1980.

Sutton-Smith, B. *Toys as culture.* New York: Gardner, 1992.

Sutton-Smith, B., & J.M. Roberts. Play, games, and sports. In *Handbook of cross-cultural psychology.* Vol. 4, *Developmental psychology,* eds. H.C. Trandis & A. Heron. Boston: Allyn & Bacon, 1981.

Sutton-Smith, B., & S. Sutton-Smith. *How to play with your children (and when not to).* New York: Hawthorn, 1974.

Tracy, D.M.. Toys, spatial ability, and science and mathematics achievement: Are they related? *Sex Roles* 17 (1987): 115–37.

Van Alstyne, D. *Play behavior and choice of play material of pre-school children.* Chicago: University of Chicago Press, 1932.

Vygotsky, L.S. Play and its role in the mental development of the child. In *Play: Its role in development and evolution,* eds. J. Bruner, A. Jolly, & K. Sylva. New York: Basic, 1976.

Wassermann, S. *Serious players in the primary classroom: Empowering children through active learning experiences.* New York: Teachers College Press, 1990.

Werner, H., & B. Kaplan. *Symbol formation.* New York: John Wiley & Sons, 1963.

White, B.L. *The first three years of life.* New York: Avon, 1978.

White, S.H. Some general outlines of the matrix of developmental changes between five and seven years. *Bulletin of the Orton Society* 20 (1970): 41–57.

Whiting, B.B., & C.P. Edwards. *Children of different worlds: The formation of social behavior.* Cambridge, MA: Harvard University Press, 1988.

Wortham, S.C., & J.L. Frost, eds. *Playgrounds for young children: National survey and perspectives.* Reston, VA: American Alliance for Health, Physical Education, Recreation and Dance, 1990.

Yawkey, T.D., & A.D. Pellegrini, eds. *Child's play: Developmental and applied.* Hillsdale, NJ: Erlbaum, 1984.

Yawkey, T.D., & J.A. Toro-Lopez. Examining descriptive and empirically based typologies of toys for handicapped and nonhandicapped children. *Topics in Early Childhood Special Education* 5 (1985): 47–58.

# Guide to Play Materials by Type

| Art and Craft Materials | | |
|---|---|---|
| **Age** | **Appropriate Materials** | **Developmental Considerations** |
| Older infants (9 through 12 months) | large, nontoxic crayons in bright colors and large, sturdy paper for scribbling | show emerging interest in marking paper |
| Young toddlers (1 year) | same materials as for older infants | show increasing interest in scribbling |
| Older toddlers (2 years) | all nontoxic materials (safe for putting in the mouth)<br>fingerpaint/paper, tempera paints, adjustable easel and large paper, large blunt brushes<br>sturdy crayons, Magic Markers<br>chalkboard, large chalk, eraser<br>easy-to-use blunt scissors<br>colored construction paper<br>playdough, clay | show increasing interest in color variations and using simple art materials<br>are interested in process rather than product |
| Preschool and kindergarten children (3 through 5 years) | all nontoxic materials (safe for putting in the mouth)<br>more and smaller crayons, markers, and chalk as child gets older<br>colored pencils<br>variety of drawing, painting, and construction papers<br>blunt-end scissors<br>paste/glue<br>collage materials<br>paintbrushes of various sizes<br>watercolor paints<br>block printing equipment<br>clay/dough and tools for modeling<br>workbench, hammer, nails, saw (with careful supervision) | are interested in a wide variety of materials and gradually increase focus on product as well as process over this period |
| Primary-school children (6 through 8 years) | (all materials appropriate for younger children, plus the following)<br>art chalks and pastels<br>all art papers, sketch pads<br>all safe paste/glue<br>stencils<br>regular scissors<br>more complex printing materials<br>more complete woodworking tools (with supervision)<br>self-hardening clay, plaster of paris, papier-mâché<br>jewelry, copper, enameling equipment<br>creative sewing materials (looms, spool-knitting materials, needles and thread)<br>leather working and braiding equipment<br>beginning photography equipment | are interested in producing a product and in participating in a wide variety of art and craft activities<br>are interested in working on products and projects over extended periods<br>are interested in special art/wood-working instruction<br>are able to use an increasing variety of materials with instruction and supervision |

# Audiovisual Materials

| Age | Appropriate Materials | Developmental Considerations |
|---|---|---|
| Young infants (birth through 6 months) | soft, gentle "live" or recorded music/songs/rhythms that are soothing, simple, and repetitive (nothing loud or sudden) | respond to and may be soothed by gentle rhythms, music, and singing |
| Older infants (7 through 12 months) | same materials as for younger infants, with more simple repeating rhymes and nursery rhymes | as above, with slightly greater variety and range of sounds |
| Young toddlers (1 year) | music/songs simple enough for them to try to repeat (repetitive songs, tunes, and rhythms)<br><br>music/rhythms to move to<br><br>simple "point-to" and finger-play songs<br><br>music to play along with (using rhythm instruments) | enjoy more active participation with sounds (imitation of rhymes, "dancing," playing instruments) |
| Older toddlers (2 years) | same materials as for younger toddlers, with added complexity of music/songs/rhythms<br><br>short films/videotapes of familiar objects and events (animals, vehicles at work, etc.) | are capable of a wider range of actions for participation (in repeating songs, pointing and finger-play activities, instrument playing, movement to music) |
| Preschool and kindergarten children (3 through 5 years) | story recordings, more complex music for movement (for dancing and acting out characters), a wider variety of music for use with rhythm instruments, longer and more complex songs (including folk songs and finger-play songs)<br><br>films and videos (stories from books, about nature, about children doing familiar activities)<br><br>simple computer games and activities (with careful adult supervision) | demonstrate increasing repertoire of singing, dancing, and rhythm skills<br><br>are able to cooperate more in groups, and so find longer, more complex group and individual activities interesting<br><br>may sing in tune and enjoy group singing<br><br>can pretend to be an animal or a character (in movement to music, acting out songs or stories)<br><br>(by ages 4–5) can operate simple tape players and make their own recordings (such activities may be hard to manage in group settings) |
| Primary-school children (6 through 8 years) | simple, self-operated audiovisual equipment of various types<br><br>faster and more complex music and songs (folk dancing, introduction to orchestra, children's opera/plays)<br><br>more complex video and computer games (checkers and chess programs, target games) | enjoy operating audiovisual equipment independently and can participate in more complex group activities |

## Balls and Sports Equipment

| Age | Appropriate Materials | Developmental Considerations |
|---|---|---|
| Young infants (3 through 6 months) | clutch balls, texture and soft balls made of soft materials, with bright colors, about 5-inch diameter | use soft balls as grasping toys and may enjoy simple effects produced by shaking |
| Older infants (7 through 12 months) | transparent, chime, flutter, and action balls | enjoy the rolling motion of balls and may try to move after them<br><br>are attracted by movement and sound |
| Young toddlers (1 year) | large, light beach balls, balls with holes, ping-pong balls, footballs<br>(from about 18 months) smaller balls—larger than 1¼-inch diameter for safety | enjoy variety and will experiment with different actions of balls<br>like unusual motions<br>may roll a ball back to another |
| Older toddlers (2 years) | balls of all shapes and sizes<br>large balls (10–12 inches) to throw and catch | enjoy throwing and retrieving balls and catching and kicking larger balls |
| Preschool and kindergarten children (3 through 5 years) | balls for kicking, throwing, and catching<br>soft balls to hit with large plastic bat<br>beanbags and materials to throw at targets<br>(by age 5) jump rope, flying plastic disks | show increasing interest in activity and skill development with balls and practice "games" with simple rules (but not ready for team sports) |
| Primary-school children (6 through 7 years) | youth- or regular-size sports equipment (baseball, basketball, kickball, soccer)<br>(from about 8 years) marbles, croquet set | show beginning interest in more organized sports activities and teams (but not much emphasis on competition before age 8) |

# Books

| Age | Appropriate Materials | Developmental Considerations |
|---|---|---|
| Older infants (7 through 12 months) | 6–8-inch books—light, with 4–5 easy-to-turn, hard-to-rip pages (cloth, heavy cardboard, plastic), in color-fast, nontoxic, bright colors<br><br>books for lap reading | may show interest in pictures and manipulating pages and may enjoy adult labeling of pictures |
| Young toddlers (1 year) | cardboard books<br>(from 18 months) heavy paper pages, tactile/touch-me books<br>simple picture/storybooks, nursery rhyme books, ABC and number books | show increased interest in simple stories and rhymes, as well as manipulation of books |
| Older toddlers (2 years) | simple pop-up, dress-me, and hidden-picture books<br>more simple storybooks | are interested in larger variety of manipulable books and storybooks<br>are more able to turn paper pages and manipulate special features |
| Preschool and kindergarten children (3 through 5 years) | more complex pop-up and dress-me books<br>preschool/kindergarten story and rhyme books with pictures—age appropriate for interest as outlined below<br>*Age 3* interests: here-and-now stories, animal stories, words and rhymes, alphabet books<br>*Age 4* interests: wild stories, silly humor, familiar things, information books (farm, firehouse, zoo, etc.)<br>*Age 5* interests: realistic stories, poetry, primers, animals that behave like people | enjoy looking at books and having stories read by others<br>have interests and attention spans that change and develop with age |
| Primary-school children (6 through 8 years) | books about children, animals, and nature—also childhood classics, myths, legends, biographies, poetry, fairy tales, dictionaries (age appropriate)<br>*Age 6* interests: books about children dealing with fears, poetry, good magic<br>*Age 7* interests: fairy tales, myths, legends, fantasy vs. reality, children, animals, nature, space, planes, electricity<br>*Age 8* interests: childhood classics, biographies, fairy tales, folktales, children, animals, nature | develop individual reading preferences<br>show increasingly varied interests that may change with age<br>show varied interest in reading and skill levels, with large individual differences |

# Construction Materials

| Age | Appropriate Materials | Developmental Considerations |
| --- | --- | --- |
| Young infants (4 through 6 months) | a few soft, light, squeezable blocks (cloth or rubber, 4–6 inches), with bright colors, rounded edges, perhaps make noise if moved or shaken | use construction materials as visuals or beginning grasping toys |
| Older infants (7 through 12 months) | smaller blocks (2–4 inches) for easy stacking, with pictures of familiar objects or animals | use construction materials as grasping toys |
| Young toddlers (1 year) | more small, light blocks (cloth, wood, plastic)—15–25 for 13–18 months and 20–40 for 19–24 months (groups of children need more so that several can play)<br>(19–24 months) large, easy, plastic/vinyl press-together bricks (bristle type) | show beginning interest in combining several toys (blocks) and arranging or stacking |
| Older toddlers (2 years) | more blocks (50–60 minimum, more for groups)—kindergarten unit blocks<br>larger, lightweight blocks (hollow wood, heavy cardboard)<br>large plastic/vinyl press-together bricks (bristle and large Legos)<br>interlocking rings and screw-action sets (plastic nuts and bolts) | show beginning interest in construction (in exploring form and shape and in deliberate attempts to build something)<br>begin to use blocks in fantasy and dramatic play |
| Preschool and kindergarten children (3 through 5 years) | many blocks (80–100, more for groups) with specialized forms (curves, arches)<br>larger wood (hollow) blocks<br>many types of small construction materials (Legos, nuts and bolts and other interlocking sets, Tinkertoy and logs, etc.)—virtually all interlocking sets without tiny nuts and bolts | show major interest in large and small blocks and other construction materials<br>(ages 3–6) need increasing variety and complexity |
| Primary-school children (6 through 8 years) | large number of varied materials for complex construction, including tiny nuts, bolts, screws<br>materials for individual and group projects/models | enjoy detailed and realistic models made with blocks, bricks, and other materials<br>show desire to work on projects over extended periods<br>may be able to follow simple construction directions |

# Dolls

| Age | Appropriate Materials | Developmental Considerations |
|---|---|---|
| Young infants (birth through 6 months) | soft (cuddly) dolls (rag, beanbag) with simple, one-piece bodies, painted or molded hair, and no accessories or detachable parts<br><br>dolls that are light, washable, and able to be grasped from any angle, with bright colors and sharp contrasts—emphasis on face and especially eyes (but no movable eyes) | use dolls as visual or grasping toys<br><br>may find faces attractive (simple, clear facial features are important) |
| Older infants (7 through 12 months) | same dolls as for younger infants<br><br>most important features: face, graspability, and effect<br><br>dolls that make noise when moved or shaken (with rattles inside) | still play with dolls in the same ways as grasping toys |
| Young toddlers (1 year) | cloth dolls and vinyl or rubber baby dolls (8–13 inches) with simple clothes (need not be detachable)—no moving eyes or hair<br><br>(from about 18 months) small peg dolls (2 inches high) | use dolls possibly to support beginning pretend play and body awareness<br><br>may enjoy putting peg dolls in vehicles |
| Older toddlers (2 years) | washable baby dolls (12–15 inches) that can be fed, bathed, and diapered and have simple accessories (skin color and features represent diversity)<br><br>dolls that are easy to hold and manipulate<br><br>dress-me dolls<br><br>small peg dolls for use with cars and blocks | use dolls and other figures in dramatic play (some realistic features and simple accessories support complex role play) |
| Preschool and kindergarten children (3 through 5 years) | washable baby dolls (can have articulated limbs, simple clothes with easy closings, accessories, and special equipment (skin color, features, and clothes represent diversity)<br><br>dolls representing child (as well as baby), with skin color, features, and clothes representing diversity<br><br>small human figures to use with blocks and play scenes (representing diversity) | show great interest in dramatic and fantasy play with dolls and human figures<br><br>show more interest in detail and accessories<br><br>incorporate play figures and animals into block play |
| Primary-school children (6 through 8 years) | (at ages 6–7) larger baby dolls with clothes and lots of accessories<br><br>small human figures for fantasy scenes and models<br><br>cut-out paper dolls<br><br>(all dolls and figures with skin color, features, and clothes representing diversity) | (ages 6–8) show some continuing interest in housekeeping play with dolls in the early primary years<br><br>use small human figures in fantasy scenes and models throughout this period |

# Dressing, Lacing, and Stringing Materials

| Age | Appropriate Materials | Developmental Considerations |
|---|---|---|
| Young toddlers (1 year) | a few large beads (at least 1 inch, 10 or fewer before 18 months), and braided or plastic string (less than 12 inches long)<br><br>lacing cubes or boards with thick, blunt spindles<br><br>wood or plastic materials (unbreakable, cleanable) in bright colors | show beginning interest in these materials, with manipulation the primary interest and goal |
| Older toddlers (2 years) | cards or wooden shoe for lacing<br><br>frames/cubes for buttoning, snapping, lacing, hooking, buckling<br><br>dressing cloth books<br><br>dress-me dolls | are interested in mastering self-help skills and developing independence |
| Preschool and kindergarten children (3 through 5 years) | more and smaller (½ inch) beads in more subtle colors (gold, silver), and longer string (longer than 12 inches) with stiff point<br><br>sewing cards<br><br>(age 5) simple weaving materials, looper looms | show quickly developing skill with these materials and interest in practicing these skills |
| Primary-school children (6 through 8 years) | beads of any size and material (pottery, glass, bead jewelry kits)<br><br>sewing materials (real needle and cloth to make doll or puppet clothes)<br><br>hand looms, spool-knitting supplies, leather sewing and braiding materials | are interested in using mastered skills in producing products<br><br>find a wide range of activities and materials interesting<br><br>may use more and smaller materials |

## Games

| Age | Appropriate Materials | Developmental Considerations |
|-----|----------------------|------------------------------|
| Older toddlers (2 years) | simple games with few pieces<br>game pieces that are not too small (2–4 inches)<br>simple matching (lotto-type) games with few pairs (3–5)<br>giant (picture, color) dominoes<br>magnetic fishing games | enjoy games that they can do alone or with one other child and/or an adult |
| Preschool and kindergarten children (3 through 5 years) | more complex matching games (more pieces), including lotto<br>dominoes (picture, color, number)<br>simple card games (Concentration)<br>(4–5 years) first board games<br>picture bingo (matching letter/number bingo at about age 5)<br>games involving construction or balancing | develop ability to take turns, concentrate, attend to detail, and understand rule-based interaction supported by early games<br>can play games in which outcome is determined by chance, not strategy<br>may play with one or two peers but may have difficulty losing |
| Primary-school children (6 through 8 years) | simple guessing or deductive games, strategy games, trading games, card games, bingo, dominoes, marbles, checkers, Chinese checkers<br>word games, arithmetic games (simple adding games) | are increasingly interested in games but hate to lose<br>can play competitive games by about age 8<br>show increasing capacity for cooperative interaction and use of strategy nurtured by games (but games should have relatively few rules and not require complicated strategies) |

## Grasping Toys

| Age | Appropriate Materials | Developmental Considerations |
| --- | --- | --- |
| Young infants (3 through 6 months) | lightweight, brightly colored objects that can be easily grasped from any angle<br><br>objects requiring only simple manipulations (shaking, squeezing)<br><br>objects with sound and visual effects produced by batting/grasping<br><br>objects with interesting taste, texture, smell<br><br>toys on suction cups (when child is able to sit) | may need several (a selection of) grasping toys that are varied occasionally to maintain interest (some new, some familiar objects)<br><br>may soon develop favorites<br><br>may need to have object held out to be grasped at first and may drop object (through lack of control) and need to have it held out again (if object is not hung at a convenient, reachable play height) |
| Older infants (7 through 12 months) | objects designed for more complex action (as motor control increases), plus use of two hands and five fingers<br><br>objects that open and shut or appear and disappear | enjoy having a larger selection and variety of toys (materials can be put away for a while, then reintroduced)<br><br>need evolving complexity of toy and motor control to challenge growing capacities (although a few "favorites" may remain attractive)<br><br>(10–12 months) are interested in object displacement (including letting go and retrieving) and in small objects |
| Young toddlers (1 year) | complex grasping toys requiring complex manipulations (dials, switches, knobs, pieces fitting together) | find objects with a variety of possibilities more interesting now; may prefer "busy boxes" to simple grasping toys |

# Mirrors

| Age | Appropriate Materials | Developmental Considerations |
|---|---|---|
| Young infants (2 through 6 months) | mirrors mounted firmly on changing area, wall, crib, etc., for ease of looking<br>mirrors large enough for infant to see self and own movements<br>nonbreakable mirrors with no sharp edges | enjoy changing stimulus provided by own motions<br>are particularly interested in faces and can see own and other faces in mirror (position of mirror important for line and angle of sight) |
| Older infants (7 through 12 months) | lower, mounted, large mirrors so that infant can see whole self crawl, sit, walk, etc.<br>smaller, very sturdy mirrors to grasp and hold<br>nonbreakable mirrors with no sharp edges | show developing awareness of self and self in space (clarity of image important—avoid dim or distorted image) |
| Young toddlers (1 year) | full-length mounted mirrors for self-awareness so that child can see self dressing/dressing up (hat, scarf, etc.)<br>small, sturdy hand mirrors (with no handle)<br>nonbreakable mirrors with no sharp edges | show active interest in seeing and creating effects in wall and hand-held mirrors |
| Older toddlers (2 years) | large, mounted and small, sturdy hand mirrors (for beginning use in pretend play)<br>nonbreakable mirrors with no sharp edges | use mirrors (large and small) added to dramatic play area |
| Preschool and kindergarten children (3 through 5 years) | full-length and hand mirrors used for role play and self-awareness<br>realistic-looking hand-mirror props<br>nonbreakable mirrors with no sharp edges | incorporate mirrors into dramatic play<br>may enjoy cleaning mirrors with safe cleaner |
| Primary-school children (6 through 8 years) | more fragile wall and hand mirrors (for checking image and experimentation with mirror-image objects, etc.) | use mirrors as adults would use them—to check image presented to world |

| Mobiles/Visuals | | |
| --- | --- | --- |
| **Age** | **Appropriate Materials** | **Developmental Considerations** |
| Young infants (birth through 5 months) | visual distance—not more than about 14 inches from eyes for infants younger than 3 months, then gradually higher as focus improves<br><br>size—within visual field at appropriate distance for age<br><br>angle of object—should allow view of interesting features from infant's position and angle of vision<br><br>color/contrast—bright, primary colors and high visual contrast<br><br>features/detail—few and distinct rather than many and complex features, patterned rather than plain color stimuli, clear edges, accentuated features and pattern markers, and faces—especially focusing on the eyes<br><br>special effects—moving rather than static displays, displays accompanied by sound, movement that is not too fast or slow (or infants will not be able to follow the display visually; sudden movements could cause a startle reaction) rhythmic sounds and sounds that are not too sudden or loud | enjoy watching and tracking interesting objects and displays with the characteristics described<br><br>show interest in slow movement and gentle sounds<br><br>may lose interest in a familiar display—some features can be altered or a new display put up<br><br>have individually varying responses to effects—an effect that pleases one may provide too much or too little stimulation for another<br><br>(4–6 months) are beginning to swipe and reach—sturdier, graspable objects can be hung for self-produced interesting effects from the infants' own actions; at this point, objects can be placed appropriately for for swiping, batting, grasping, or kicking |

# Musical Instruments

| Age | Appropriate Materials | Developmental Considerations |
|---|---|---|
| Young infants (birth through 5 months) | washable rattles and bells (including wrist bells)—light, unbreakable, small (not swallowable), with no sharp edges or points, with clear sound, but not too loud<br><br>materials to listen to (birth through 2 months) then grasp (from 3 months)<br><br>musical instruments (with soft, gentle sounds/rhythms) that may be played to infants | use rattles and bells as grasping toys<br><br>enjoy special sounds (soft sounds, because sudden or loud sounds can be frightening)<br><br>enjoy singing and music for listening from the earliest ages |
| Older infants (7 through 12 months) | rubber or wood blocks that rattle or tinkle when shaken, banged, or squeezed<br><br>safe rattles and bells | still use materials as grasping toys<br><br>enjoy items that are easy to handle, with pleasing sounds |
| Young toddlers (1 year) | beginning simple rhythm instruments with bells or rattles (sturdy, rounded, cleanable)<br><br>(from 18 months) simple, sturdy beginning drums<br><br>simple hand-cranked music box<br><br>sturdy, safe instruments (that can be banged, dropped, etc.) | respond increasingly to rhythms and varied sounds, and show growing interest in creating interesting effects |
| Older toddlers (2 years) | more kinds of rhythm instruments (tambourine, sand blocks, triangle, rhythm sticks)<br><br>instruments with no sharp edges or points | are increasingly interested in imitating and experimenting with musical sounds |
| Preschool and kindergarten children (3 through 5 years) | more kinds of rhythm instruments (castanets, xylophone)<br><br>other instruments—horns, whistles, harmonica, ocarina, recorder (wind instruments for individual use only) | enjoy hearing and making music alone or in groups (rhythm bands, singing, dancing)<br><br>benefit from a variety of instruments for experimentation |
| Primary-school children (6 through 8 years) | (usually age 7–8) instruments for music lessons (piano, autoharp, recorder, flute, violin, horn) | can participate in group music activities (singing, playing with individually owned recorders)<br><br>vary in musical interest and skill |

# Outdoor and Gym Equipment

| Age | Appropriate Materials | Developmental Considerations |
|---|---|---|
| Older infants (7 through 12 months) | for infants who can sit unsupported: soft, low infant swings with back, sides, and front bar (constant supervision required)<br>for infants who can crawl and climb: low climbing platforms and large foam blocks (soft, regularly cleaned) to climb on | enjoy being pushed in swings and climbing over low obstacles, but careful supervision is necessary |
| Young toddlers (1 year) | low steps and slides with hand rails<br>simple, very low wooden, plastic, or foam climb-on structures<br>soft (rubber, canvas) swings<br>tunnels | delight in using their developing gross motor abilities in many different types of activities<br>are not good judges of danger or their own abilities and need to be carefully supervised |
| Older toddlers (2 years) | stationary, simple climbing structures<br>low slides with sides<br>low, soft (rubber, canvas) swings (children still need to be pushed)<br>tunnels | show eagerness to try ever-more-challenging gross motor actions and may use them in pretend play<br>need constant supervision, as they are not deterred by heights and dangerous situations |
| Preschool and kindergarten children (3 through 5 years) | climbing structures with lots of moving parts (swings, ropes, bars, ladders, hanging rings, and enclosures)<br>slides without side rails<br>flat swing seats (soft)<br>small seesaws<br>structures with potential for role-play activities | enjoy vigorous gross motor play and are increasingly skilled in using a variety of equipment<br>increasingly incorporate gross motor activities into dramatic play—games and equipment can support this use |
| Primary-school children (6 through 8 years) | more complex and higher equipment sets, with rings, bars, ropes, and poles (for "acrobatics")<br>equipment that is regularly checked for safety (may get hard use) | enjoy testing their skills and may compete in performance of them |

## Pattern-Making Materials

| Age | Appropriate Materials | Developmental Considerations |
|---|---|---|
| Young toddlers (1 year) | a few large, brightly colored wood or plastic pegs that the child may put into holes in a board (wood, foam, plastic)<br>pegs that are too large to fit in the mouth | are primarily interested in manipulation of materials and developing manual skills |
| Older toddler (2 years) | pegboards (wood, foam, plastic) with large pegs in a variety of colors<br>magnetic boards with shapes<br>color cubes (color forms from 30 months) | begin to show interest in pattern and sequence<br>need large, easily handled pieces |
| Preschool and kindergarten children (3 through 5 years) | (by age 5) pegboards with smaller pegs (smaller than 2 inches)<br>number boards with pegs and pegboard villages<br>color, shape, and design materials of wood, plastic, paper, felt, metal (magnetic)<br>mosaic blocks, felt boards, plastic shapes<br>block printing equipment | show great interest in design of all kinds<br>develop increasing skill in pattern making<br>can now handle smaller pieces (1–2 inches) |
| Primary-school children (6 through 8 years) | beads, ceramic tiles, cloth, cardboard, wood, plastic, etc. (virtually all materials for pattern making)—art materials for design products | are interested in more complicated patterns and designs<br>show great interest in producing a permanent product |

# Play Scenes

| Age | Appropriate Materials | Developmental Considerations |
|---|---|---|
| Young toddlers (1 year) | a few small (3–5-inch) figures, animals, vehicles, or peg dolls (2–4 inches) and buildings/enclosures (with easy access to interior)<br><br>lightweight rubber, plastic, or wooden objects in bright colors<br><br>objects realistic enough to be familiar<br><br>materials for simple familiar scenes (only 4–6 pieces, all with parts too large to be swallowed) | use play scenes to support beginning fantasy play (playing alone or in parallel play) |
| Older toddlers (2 years) | small representations of people and animals, with a few vehicles and/or enclosures (for rooms, barns, garages, etc.)<br><br>materials with which to make scenes of familiar activities (pieces must be very sturdy with no sharp or swallowable parts) | use play scenes to support developing fantasy play and fine motor coordination<br><br>can incorporate more pieces into fantasy play and enjoy moving parts (doors that open, sliding doors, cranks) |
| Preschool and kindergarten children (3 through 5 years) | wide range of human and animal figures, vehicles, and optional simple props (road signs, fences, furniture) with which to create scenes<br><br>simple, generic enclosures (or children can use blocks or other construction materials to make fantasy settings, such as buildings, fences, furniture, roads, etc.)<br><br>materials from which to create favorite scenes (garages, roads, farms, airports, space) | typically use play scenes for fantasy and dramatic play with one or several other children in group settings<br><br>often use materials with blocks or with sand or water |
| Primary-school children (6 through 8 years) | more pieces for play scenes (although children are also more capable of making props and details for scenes with blocks or other construction materials)<br><br>materials from which to create more grown-up scenes and themes | (ages 6 and 7) show interest in creating more detailed scenes to be used and added to over days or weeks (can make many parts and details themselves)<br><br>(by age 8) may be more interested in producing permanent models<br><br>can create realistic models of curriculum topics with play scene materials |

## Puppets

| Age | Appropriate Materials | Developmental Considerations |
| --- | --- | --- |
| Older infants (7 through 12 months) | hand and finger puppets operated by an adult (with simple features, bright colors)<br><br>sturdy, safe materials (if children touch or handle objects) | display no true puppet play, but puppets may facilitate interaction with adults |
| Young toddlers (1 year) | (from 18 months) sturdy, washable, lightweight, small hand puppets—8–12 inches in size and sized to toddler's small hand | use puppets in the same way as stuffed animals<br><br>show particular interest in contrasting facial features and eyes |
| Older toddlers (2 years) | simple hand puppets representing familiar figures | as above, and may begin to exhibit simple interactive play with adults using puppets |
| Preschool and kindergarten children (3 through 5 years) | hand puppets of all sizes, including sock or mitten puppets—very sturdy and representing diversity<br><br>finger puppets (wood, cloth)<br><br>simple puppet theater | increasingly enjoy puppet play throughout this period for acting out own stories<br><br>enjoy simple "theater" (although this can be constructed of blocks, shelves, etc.) |
| Primary-school children (6 through 8 years) | puppets with arms, jointed puppets, rod puppets, puppets made with hard materials—children are also capable of making a variety of puppets<br><br>no marionettes yet<br><br>more elaborate puppet theater with curtains and scenery (may be constructed by children) | are increasingly interested in the presented "play" and in details and special effects<br><br>act out familiar stories and, later, scripted plays |

## Push and Pull Toys

| Age | Appropriate Materials | Developmental Considerations |
|---|---|---|
| Older infants (7 through 12 months) | lightweight objects that are easy to grasp and push (5–7 inches), with large wheels or rollers<br><br>simple, undetailed objects with bright colors and no small or removable parts<br><br>objects that make noise or have parts that move as object is moved | may enjoy crawling and pushing floor toys with wheels or rollers, especially those that produce interesting sights or sounds<br><br>have limited balance and skill, so safety is a primary consideration—materials should be easily controllable and have no sharp parts or edges to fall on |
| Young toddlers (1 year) | heavier toys—broad based, with a low center of gravity (to prevent tipping)<br><br>push toys with rigid rods and handles for toddlers who walk<br><br>toys with interesting sounds and sights<br><br>(from about 18 months) simple, sturdy carriages and wagons with rounded edges (wood, plastic—no metal) | (beginning walkers) like to walk and push things that help them keep their balance (materials to support walking should be sturdy enough to provide some support for the child and should be very stable)<br><br>like to push containers that hold other materials and push or pull toys that produce interesting effects when maneuvered (pull toys should have short strings to prevent entangling and tripping) |
| Older toddlers (2 years) | pretend materials for pushing/pulling that are sturdy but light, with rounded edges for safe handling<br><br>models of objects used by adults (lawn mower, vacuum cleaner, shopping cart)<br><br>maneuverable, low objects with large wheels, rounded edges<br><br>(from about 36 months) simple, small wheelbarrows | love to pretend, using push or pull toys that resemble real equipment |
| Preschool and kindergarten children (3 through 5 years) | larger materials with more detail | (approaching age 6) show declining interest in push/pull toys (favor ride-on materials) except for full-size wagons<br><br>now use materials of this type for dramatic play or real work (typically cleaning)<br><br>increasingly prefer equipment that really works |

| Puzzles | | |
|---|---|---|
| **Age** | **Appropriate Materials** | **Developmental Considerations** |
| Older infants (7 through 12 months) | 2–3-piece lightweight wood or plastic puzzles, with pieces too large to swallow<br>unbreakable, cleanable pieces with rounded edges and bright colors/high contrast | use "puzzle" materials as grasping toys (any simple pre-puzzles used should meet the requirements of grasping toys) |
| Young toddlers (1 year) | simple fitting toys and puzzle blocks with large, firmly attached knobs on pieces<br>(from about 18 months) 3–5-piece fit-ins (shape-sorting sets, form boards, puzzles, nesting items) | show interest in simple fitting-together toys, which develop their skills |
| Older toddlers (2 years) | (25–30 months) 4–5-piece wood or plastic fit-in puzzles<br>(30–36 months) 6–12-piece fit-ins<br>puzzles that have clarity of form and firmly attached knobs | show increasing interest in simple form puzzles<br>benefit from variety, for interest and choice |
| Preschool and kindergarten children (3 through 5 years) | 12–50-piece puzzles (cardboard, as well as wood and plastic)<br>jigsaw as well as fit-in puzzles (from about 43 months)<br>puzzle clocks, number/letter and layered puzzles | enjoy doing puzzles and may do one after another<br>have individual differences in skill and interest, so they benefit from variety in type and number of pieces |
| Primary-school children (6 through 8 years) | 50–100-piece jigsaw puzzles (up to 500 pieces from age 8)<br>three-dimensional puzzles<br>map puzzles | may enjoy the challenge of large puzzles done over several days or weeks<br>display great individual differences in interest and skill |

# Ride-On Equipment

| Age | Appropriate Materials | Developmental Considerations |
|---|---|---|
| Young toddlers (1 year) | (for youngest toddlers) casters and no steering capability<br><br>low, small, and well-balanced objects with easily moved wheels and no pedals<br><br>solid wood or heavy-duty molded plastic objects in bright colors<br><br>representations of animals and ride-ons that make noise and have storage bins<br><br>equipment with stability (important for safety) | enjoy this type of equipment for gross motor play, indoors or outdoors, so several should be available (depending on size of group)<br><br>prefer special effects (sounds or appearance), but these may make an item harder to share |
| Older toddlers (2 years) | first rocking/bouncing horses—stable, with confined rocking arc (child's toes should touch floor)<br><br>more realistic-looking ride-ons | increasingly enjoy ride-on materials as skill in using them increases<br><br>(2½–3 years) show emerging ability to pedal, using ride-ons with 10-inch wheels<br><br>(as children are able to move large distances and use pedals) may find using some of this equipment indoors confining or disruptive, so outdoor use is more desirable |
| Preschool and kindergarten children (3 through 5 years) | plastic or metal ride-ons, such as tricycles (about 13-inch wheels for 3–4-year-olds)<br><br>(4–5 years) low-slung tricycles and scooters<br><br>realistic ride-ons, such as cars, trucks, and horses (but these can create problems regarding sharing in group settings) | enjoy these materials for both gross motor skill building and pretend play<br><br>(by age 5) may be highly skilled and may want first bicycles (which are not easily handled in most school outdoor settings)<br><br>now prefer smooth, safe outdoor surfaces |
| Primary-school children (6 through 8 years) | two-wheeler bicycles—metal with foot brakes (hand brakes at 7 to 8 years); bikes are no longer school equipment at this age | often show great interest in bike riding, but bicycles should now be used outside school grounds |

# Role-Play Materials

| Age | Appropriate Materials | Developmental Considerations |
|---|---|---|
| Older infants (7 through 12 months) | dolls and stuffed animals | use items for grasping and cuddling, not for role play |
| Young toddlers (1 year) | toy telephone, housecleaning sets, unbreakable dishes<br>(from 18 months) unbreakable pots and pans, toy lawn mower and vacuum cleaner<br>purses, shoes (for dress-up)<br>(from 18 months) hats, ties, scarves<br>(from 18 months) doll bottle, feeding equipment, blanket<br>baby carriages (to push and ride in)<br>(from 18 months) child-size wood cradle/bed, table and chair, rocking chair | use materials for supporting beginning fantasy play (sturdiness is important) |
| Older toddlers (2 years) | pots and pans with covers, cutlery<br>housecleaning set, including broom, dustpan, dustcloth, mop, carpet sweeper<br>dress-up clothes, gloves, vests, suitcases<br>doll clothes with Velcro or big buttons<br>doll stroller, shopping cart, doll tub, laundry tub and clothespins, stove, sink, cupboard, ironing board and iron | use materials for supporting developing fantasy and role play |
| Preschool and kindergarten children (3 through 5 years) | props for roles* (dress-ups, medical kits, cash register, play money, and material for playing train, plane, spaceship, office, school, etc.) (culturally appropriate for group)<br>cooking and dishwashing materials<br>doll highchair, bassinet, brushes and combs, more elaborate doll clothes<br>play store, puppet stage (perhaps made with blocks) | show great interest in role play with a variety of materials<br>can use fantasy and role-play materials to support any number of themes woven into the overall curriculum |
| Primary-school children (6 through 8 years) | role-play equipment that really works (real cooking equipment, real camera, real sewing equipment, etc.)<br>adult-role dress-ups, makeup/disguise materials for performances<br>props for shows and dramatic performances (these can be made by the children) | more frequently use role-play materials as means rather than ends—to support model building, projects, and plays or dramatic performances in school settings |

*Props that are weapons (guns, bows and arrows, swords, etc.) are excluded because they are not considered safe or appropriate for group play.

# Sand and Water Play Materials

| Age | Appropriate Materials | Developmental Considerations |
|---|---|---|
| Older infants (7 through 12 months) | small floating objects—light, easily grasped (4–6 inches), and constructed to float easily and right themselves in the water<br><br>objects with bright colors and simple (not detailed) designs | enjoy water and floating objects<br><br>use objects as grasping toys and may mouth them (sponges are not safe, because children may bite off pieces) |
| Young toddlers (1 year) | representations of objects<br>(from about 18 months) more materials with which to explore properties of water (funnels, colanders, sprinkling cans, containers for filling/emptying, multiple parts for nesting or linking, or removable peg dolls or animals) and simple water activity centers (with hinges, push buttons, levers of 2–4 inches)<br><br>small sand tools (shovels, pails, rakes with blunt teeth) | enjoy small floating objects and actively explore with water<br><br>find water and sand interesting elements in themselves<br><br>enjoy simple objects for exploring properties of water and sand (filling and emptying, pouring, sifting, floating, etc.) |
| Older toddlers (2 years) | small people/animal figures for fantasy play in sand or water<br><br>boats (wooden, plastic, rubber)<br><br>sand/water mills, simple sieves and strainers<br><br>larger sand tools (18 inches and larger to be used while standing up) | enjoy sand and water play as favorite activities<br><br>can successfully use more varieties of materials for exploring sand and water<br><br>are interested also in materials for fantasy play in sand or water |
| Preschool and kindergarten children (3 through 5 years) | water pumps, tubes, funnels, measuring containers for experimenting in sand or water<br><br>human, animal, vehicle objects for fantasy play in sand or water<br><br>sand molds<br><br>bubble liquid | use materials for experimentation, as well as exploration and fantasy play<br><br>interest in experimental "sink and float" activities |
| Primary-school children (6 through 8 years) | sand and water | use sand and water as media for constructing models (of rivers, lakes, land forms) and for other activities |

# Specific Skill-Development Materials

| Age | Appropriate Materials | Developmental Considerations |
|---|---|---|
| Older infants (7 through 12 months) | materials that produce effects—activity boxes and simple pop-up materials<br><br>objects that are interesting to explore (texture pads) or manipulate (stacking rings, nesting cups, objects in containers)—3–5 pieces, 2–4 inches each, of lightweight material (wood, plastic, cloth), easily graspable | use manipulatives for development of manual skills, exploration, and cause–effect awareness |
| Young toddlers (1 year) | round nesting and fitting materials<br>simple stacking materials—no order necessary<br>hidden-object toys—pop-up and "surprise" boxes (now with lids, doors, dials, switches, knobs)<br>(from about 18 months) activity boxes with more complex mechanisms (turning knob or dial or simple key), simple shape sorters, cylinder blocks, 4–5-piece stacking materials, square nesting materials<br>pounding/hammering toys<br>pegboards with a few large pegs<br>(from about 20 months) simple matching and lotto materials | show great interest in these types of materials, which are useful for developing both fine motor skills and understanding of the physical world (through nesting, stacking, matching) |
| Older toddlers (2 years) | 5–10 pieces to nest/stack; one-turn, screw-on (barrel) nesting sets<br>simple lock boxes<br>matching and sorting materials (by color, picture, shape), color/picture dominoes, lotto<br>feel bag/box, smell jar | demonstrate skills/interest as above, with increasing complexity of action and concept and more pieces to nest, stack, and match<br>need materials with simple, clear criteria for early concept learning |

# Specific Skill-Development Materials (cont'd)

| Age | Appropriate Materials | Developmental Considerations |
|---|---|---|
| Preschool and kindergarten children (3 through 5 years) | 10 or more pieces to nest/stack<br><br>matching, sorting, grading materials (by color, shape, picture, number, size, letter, concept)<br><br>simple machines (pendulum, lever, gears, pulley, inclined plane)<br><br>concrete counting and seriating materials (number rods, number dominoes, number boards with pegs)<br><br>simple geometrical concept and fraction materials (mosaic shapes, puzzles)<br><br>measuring materials (balance scales, graded cups for liquid/sand, etc.)<br><br>science materials (prism, magnifying glass, color paddles, stethoscope, plant/body-part models)<br><br>natural materials to sort (rocks, shells, seeds, etc.)<br><br>plants and animals to care for and observe<br><br>print-making materials (shapes, numbers, letters)<br><br>beginning computer software (simple programs for drawing, sequencing, learning about the computer, and activities with shapes, quantities) | show increasing interest in complexity of action and concept and increasing goal—as well as process—orientation<br><br>enjoy learning about many things and may show spontaneous interest in playing with a variety of play and learning materials<br><br>benefit from both open-ended materials for experimenting and self-correcting materials |
| Primary-school children (6 through 8 years) | more complex printing materials, typewriters, materials for making books<br><br>math manipulatives, fraction and geometrical materials<br><br>measuring materials (balance scales, rulers, graded measuring containers)<br><br>science materials, including models (visible woman/man), land and plant forms, body parts, large-screen microscope, prisms, weather materials (barometer, anemometer)<br><br>geography puzzles and maps<br><br>natural materials to examine/classify<br><br>plants and animals to care for/study<br><br>computer programs for language arts, number, concept development, problem solving, simple programming, word processing, music | show interest in the world around them and are curious about many things<br><br>benefit from well-chosen, concrete materials that support understanding and interest in learning |

# Stuffed Toys/Play Animals

| Age | Appropriate Materials | Developmental Considerations |
|---|---|---|
| Young infants (birth through 6 months) | small, plush animals (8–12 inches) and grab-on soft toys, with permanently attached eyes and noses and no whiskers, ribbons, bells, or buttons<br><br>animals that are washable (plush, soft vinyl, cloth) and not too hairy (should not shed)<br><br>stuffed toys in bright, primary colors, with bright, contrasting eyes—simple design, with emphasis on face and eyes<br><br>toys with a soft sound (internal rattle, bell) | use these objects as visual or grasping toys, but find the "face" and softness attractive |
| Older infants (7 through 12 months) | stuffed animals with characteristics the same as for younger infants, plus very big soft toys to be leaned on or banged<br><br>soft rubber or vinyl animals (6–8 inches)<br><br>materials that are easy to clean (important if used by more than one infant) | as above, with increased interest in softness and cuddliness (special cuddly materials brought from home may comfort infant) |
| Young toddlers (1 year) | soft, cuddly, floppy animals easy to carry around in one hand or arm (easily washable)<br><br>rubber or vinyl animals for beginning pretend play and language labeling | may develop a special fondness for a specific stuffed toy and may want to keep it close (will not want to share a favorite stuffed toy) |
| Older toddlers (2 years) | sturdy wood, rubber, vinyl, or plastic play animals (zoo, farm, aquatic)<br><br>mother and baby animal combinations | use animals in pretend play with simple accessories and for language labeling |
| Preschool and kindergarten children (3 through 5 years) | increased number and variety of sturdy wood, rubber, vinyl, and plastic animals, including reptiles and dinosaurs | use play animals in dramatic play with blocks and in fantasy play scenes |
| Primary-school children (6 through 8 years) | a variety of small play animals for use in play scenes and models | incorporate materials into constructed scenes or models |

# Transportation Toys

| Age | Appropriate Materials | Developmental Considerations |
|---|---|---|
| Older infants (7 through 12 months) | push cars—simple, one-piece cars with big wheels for easy pushing (soft plastic, rubber, or vinyl—no hard plastic or metal, and wood is too heavy)<br><br>vehicles that produce sound when moved | use vehicles as grasping and push toys<br><br>need lightweight vehicles<br><br>prefer objects that produce interesting effects when pushed |
| Young toddlers (1 year) | medium-size (6–8 inches) or smaller (4–6 inches) familiar vehicles (cars, trains, airplanes) made of wood, rubber, or plastic<br><br>push cars and simple push/pull "trains" (with 1–3 cars, very simple coupling mechanism, and no tracks)<br><br>(from 18 months) vehicles with more working parts (doors, hoods, propellers, dumpers), and vehicles pulled with cords<br><br>(18—24 months) simple vehicles (trucks) that can carry other objects<br><br>unbreakable vehicles with no sharp edges | enjoy simple actions of vehicles and motor actions of moving them<br><br>prefer familiar-looking, recognizable vehicles |
| Older toddlers (2 years) | little wood or plastic vehicles (3–4 inches) for play scenes, and larger vehicles (12–15 inches) for pushing<br><br>abstract, unpainted, solid wood trucks, including larger ride-on type<br><br>large plastic trucks with simple figures/accessories and working parts<br><br>small wood or plastic trains (no tracks)<br><br>very sturdy vehicles with no small swallow-able parts and no sharp edges | show growing interest in groups of smaller vehicles for fantasy play |
| Preschool and kindergarten children (3 through 5 years) | large and smaller cars and trucks (3–36 inches) of wood or sturdy plastic (not metal collectables for groups of children)<br><br>work machines (trucks with moving parts)<br><br>small wood or plastic trains with simple or block "tracks" | enjoy vehicles of all kinds and sizes for fantasy and dramatic play<br><br>often use vehicles in conjunction with blocks |
| Primary-school children (6 through 8 years) | small collectable vehicles (but these are not practical for school settings)<br><br>vehicles that children construct at a workbench or with construction materials | show growing interest in collections and prefer detail in materials and manipulation; however, these materials are not practical in school settings<br><br>may use simple representations in scenes or models |

# Information about NAEYC

## NAEYC is . . .

. . . a membership-supported organization of people committed to fostering the growth and development of children from birth through age 8. Membership is open to all who share a desire to serve and act on behalf of the needs and rights of young children.

## NAEYC provides . . .

. . . educational services and resources to adults who work with and for children, including

- *Young Children, the* journal for early childhood educators
- **Books, posters, brochures,** and **videos** to expand your knowledge and commitment to young children, with topics including infants, curriculum, research, discipline, teacher education, and parent involvement
- An **Annual Conference** that brings people from all over the country to share their expertise and advocate on behalf of children and families
- **Week of the Young Child** celebrations sponsored by NAEYC Affiliate Groups across the nation to call public attention to the needs and rights of children and families
- **Insurance plans** for individuals and programs
- **Public affairs information** for knowledgeable advocacy efforts at all levels of government and through the media
- The **National Academy of Early Childhood Programs,** a voluntary accreditation system for high-quality programs for children
- The **National Institute for Early Childhood Professional Development,** providing resources and services to improve professional preparation and development of early childhood educators
- **Young Children International** to promote international communication and information exchanges

**For free information about membership, publications, or other NAEYC services . . .**

- call NAEYC at 202-232-8777 or 800-424-2460,
- or write to the National Association for the Education of Young Children, 1509 16th Street, NW, Washington, DC 20036-1426.